Other Works by **Harold Pinter** Published by Grove Press

The Birthday Party *and* The Room

The Caretaker *and* The Dumb Waiter

Three Plays (The Collection; A Slight Ache; The Dwarfs)

The Homecoming

The Lover, Tea Party, *and* The Basement

A Night Out, Night School, Revue Sketches: Early Plays

Mac (A Memoir)

Landscape *and* Silence

Old Times

Five Screenplays (The Servant; The Pumpkin Eater; The Quiller Memorandum [The Berlin Memorandum]; Accident; The Go-Between)

No Man's Land

Complete Works: One (The Birthday Party; The Room; The Dumb Waiter; A Slight Ache; A Night Out; The Black and White; The Examination)

Complete Works: Two (The Caretaker; Night School; The Dwarfs; The Collection; The Lover; Five Revue Sketches [Trouble in the Works; The Black and White; Request Stop; Last to Go; Special Offer])

THE
PROUST
SCREENPLAY

À LA RECHERCHE DU TEMPS PERDU

THE
PROUST
SCREENPLAY
BY
HAROLD PINTER

WITH
THE
COLLABORATION
OF
JOSEPH LOSEY
AND
BARBARA BRAY

GROVE PRESS, INC., NEW YORK

First Edition 1977
First Printing 1977
ISBN: 0-394-42202-3
Grove Press ISBN: 0-8021-0138-0
Library of Congress Catalog Card Number: 77-72676

First Evergreen Edition 1977
Second Printing 1978
ISBN: 0-394-17018-0
Grove Press ISBN: 0-8021-4083-1
Library of Congress Catalog Card Number: 77-72676

Manufactured in the United States of America

Distributed by Random House, Inc., New York

GROVE PRESS, INC., 196 West Houston Street, New York, N.Y. 10014

To Joe and Barbara

INTRODUCTION

Early in 1972 Nicole Stephane, who owned the film rights to À *la Recherche du Temps Perdu*, asked Joseph Losey if he would like to work on a film version of the book. He asked me if I was interested. We had worked together on three films up to that point: *The Servant, Accident,* and *The Go-Between.*

I had read only *Du Côté de Chez Swann,* the first volume of the work, many years before. I expressed great interest in the idea, met Joe, and Nicole Stephane, and agreed to go ahead. I also proposed that Barbara Bray, who was for many years script editor for BBC Radio and whom I knew to be a Proustian authority, join us in the venture as advisor. Joe and Barbara met and agreed to this.

For three months I read À *la Recherche du Temps Perdu* every day. I took hundreds of notes while reading but was left at the end quite baffled as to how to approach a task of such magnitude. The one thing of which I was certain was that it would be wrong to attempt to make a film centered around one or two volumes—*La Prisonnière* or *Sodome et Gomorrhe,* for example. If the thing was to be done at all, one would have to try to distill the whole work, to incorporate the major themes of the book into an integrated whole. With this Joe and Barbara agreed. We decided that the architecture of the film should be based on two main and contrasting principles: one, a movement, chiefly narrative, toward disillusion, and the other, more intermittent, toward revelation, rising to where time that was lost is found, and fixed forever in art.

Proust wrote *Du Côté de Chez Swann* first and *Le Temps Retrouvé,* the last volume, second. He then wrote the rest. The relationship between the first volume and the last seemed to us the crucial one. The whole book is, as it were, contained in the last volume. When Marcel, in *Le Temps Retrouvé*, says that he is now able to start his work, he has already written it. We have just read it. Somehow this remarkable conception had to be found again in another form. We knew we could in no sense *rival* the work. But could we be true to it?

It would take much too long now to go into the details of how and why we took the range of decisions, including the sacrifice of characters, revealed in the screenplay. They were dictated by the structure previously decided upon. We evolved a working plan and I plunged in the deep end on the basis of it. The subject was Time. In *Le Temps Retrouvé*, Marcel, in his forties, hears again the garden bell of his childhood. His childhood, long forgotten, is suddenly present within him, but his consciousness of himself as a child, his memory of the experience, is more real, more acute than the experience itself. For months I wrote and discussed the results regularly with my colleagues.

In the summer of 1972 we made a number of trips: to Illiers, to Cabourg, to Paris, and steeped ourselves in the Proustian locations. In November the screenplay was completed. It was long and clearly very expensive. I cut twenty-four pages, which in fact I thought all to the good, and at the beginning of 1973 the revised version existed and was final. This is the version published here.

Working on *À la Recherche du Temps Perdu* was the best working year of my life.

We then all tried to get the money to make the film. Up to this point the film has not been made.

Harold Pinter
May 1977

THE
PROUST
SCREENPLAY

1. *Yellow screen. Sound of a garden gate bell.*

2. *Open countryside, a line of trees, seen from a railway carriage. The train is still. No sound. Quick fade out.*

3. *Momentary yellow screen.*

4. *The sea, seen from a high window, a towel hanging on a towel rack in foreground. No sound. Quick fade out.*

5. *Momentary yellow screen.*

6. *Venice. A window in a palazzo, seen from a gondola. No sound. Quick fade out.*

7. *Momentary yellow screen.*

8. *The dining room at Balbec. No sound. Empty.*

9. EXT. THE HOUSE OF THE PRINCE DE GUER-MANTES. PARIS. 1921. AFTERNOON.

   > *In long shot a middle-aged man (*MARCEL*) walks towards the* PRINCE DE GUERMANTES*'s house.*
   >
   > *His posture is hunched, his demeanor one of defeat.*
   >
   > *Many carriages, a few cars, a crowd of chauffeurs. Realistic sound.*

10. INT. LIBRARY. THE PRINCE DE GUERMANTES'S HOUSE. 1921.

   > *A waiter inadvertently knocks a spoon against a plate.*
   >
   > MARCEL, *large in foreground, looks up.*

11. INT. DRAWING ROOM. THE PRINCE DE GUER-MANTES'S HOUSE. 1921.

   > *The drawing room doors open.*

The camera enters with MARCEL, *who hesitates.*

Hundreds of faces, some of which turn towards him, grotesquely made up, grotesquely old.

A tumult of voices.

12. *The sea from the window. Silent.*

13. *Spoon hitting plate.*

14. *Continue* MARCEL'*s progress into the drawing room. Voices. Faces. The wigs and makeup, combined with the extreme age of those who with difficulty stand, sit, gesture, laugh, give the impression of grotesque fancy dress.*

15. *In the library,* MARCEL, *a glass by his side, wipes his lips with a stiff napkin, which crackles.*

16. *Venice. Window in a palazzo. Silent.*

17. *In the drawing room, a group of very old women, talking.*

18. *Water pipes in the library.*

   The shrill noise of water running through the pipes.

19. *Silent countryside from the railway carriage.*

20. EXT. THE HOUSE OF THE PRINCE DE GUER-MANTES. 1921.

   A car swerves to avoid MARCEL.
   He steps back, trips on the cobbles.
   Chauffeur shouts.

21. *The dining room at Balbec. Silent.*

22. *Yellow screen.*

   The camera pulls back to discover that the yellow

screen is actually a patch of yellow wall in a painting.

The painting is Vermeer's View of Delft.

23. MARCEL (37) *in his room at a sanatorium, sitting motionless as an owl.*

24. INT. THE DRAWING ROOM. THE PRINCE DE GUERMANTES'S HOUSE. 1921.

> *No sound track.*
> *Old people chattering soundlessly.*
> MARCEL *stands detached from them.*
> *The sound of a garden gate bell heard, becoming gently insistent.*
>
> (*The tempo of the next sequence quickens, and the bell continues over it, irregularly.*)

25. MARCEL, *in his twenties, in his hotel room at Balbec, bending over his boots, grief-stricken.*

26. *Three church steeples, seen from a moving carriage, at sunset. They seem to be dancing together in the last rays of the sun.*

27. *Three trees, seen from a moving carriage, at noon. Although the carriage is moving away from them, the trees give the impression of following it.*

28. MARCEL *bending over his boots.*

29. *The trees.*

30. *The steeples.*

31. *Flash of yellow screen. Music of Vinteuil.*

32. *Quick shot of the garden gate at Combray. Very dim.*

33. *The steeples.*

34. *Calm, still shot of the garden gate.*

        The bell is slightly shaking but silent.

        (NOTE: *In the preceding opening sequence, all scenes in the drawing room of the* PRINCE DE GUERMANTES'S *house to be shot on color stock in black and white.*)

35. INT. MARCEL'S ROOM. COMBRAY HOUSE. 1888. EVENING.

        MARCEL, *a boy of eight, is sitting on the bed, in his nightshirt. He is writing laboriously. He finishes writing and puts the piece of paper in an envelope.*

36. EXT. THE GARDEN. COMBRAY HOUSE. EARLIER IN THE EVENING.

        MARCEL, *his* FATHER (42), MOTHER (33), *and* GRANDMOTHER (56) *sitting with* DR. PERCEPIED (50).

DR. PERCEPIED

Well, I must be going. I have to look in to see Monsieur Vinteuil. Not in the best of health, poor man.

FATHER

Mmmnn.

DR. PERCEPIED

His daughter's friend is staying with them again, apparently.

FATHER (grimly)

Is she?

DR. PERCEPIED

Yes. She's a music teacher.

MOTHER

But Monsieur Vinteuil is a music teacher himself.

DR. PERCEPIED

His daughter prefers to be taught by her friend.

6

Apparently. (*He bends forward to speak in a lower voice.*) Of course some people say it's not music she teaches his daughter, that Monsieur Vinteuil must be blind—

FATHER *coughs, glances at* MARCEL.

DR. PERCEPIED
But every time you pass the house the piano is tinkling away, tinkling away. It's a regular music box. Too much music, in my opinion. Sending Monsieur Vinteuil to his grave.

Pause.

GRANDMOTHER
Marcel looks tired.

FATHER
Yes, come on, off to bed. We said good-night to you hours ago. Isn't Swann a little late? What time are we dining?

DR. PERCEPIED
Charming man, Monsieur Swann. I was called in to see his wife yesterday. She had a slight migraine.

Pause.

FATHER (*abruptly, to* MARCEL)
Come on, come on, how many times do I have to tell you? Go to bed.

MARCEL *stands, goes to his* MOTHER, *leans forward to kiss her.*

FATHER
No, no, leave your mother alone. You've said good-night to one another. That's enough. All this fuss is ridiculous. Go upstairs.

37. *THE BACKDOOR OF THE HOUSE. GARDEN IN BACKGROUND.*

As MARCEL *enters the door:*

7

DR. PERCEPIED

Monsieur Swann is dining with you alone, I gather?

FATHER

Alone. Yes.

38. *INT. COMBRAY HOUSE.*

MARCEL *walks slowly up the stairs. The kitchen door opens.* FRANÇOISE *(late 40s) looks up.*

FRANÇOISE

That's right. Off to bed. How was your chocolate cake?

MARCEL *does not reply.* FRANÇOISE *grunts, closes door.*

39. *EXT. THE GARDEN GATE.*

The bell rings, two peals.
SWANN *enters. He is forty.*

GRANDMOTHER *walks across the grass towards him.*
FATHER *stands up in background.*

GRANDMOTHER

Good evening, Monsieur Swann.

40. *INT. MARCEL'S BEDROOM.*

FRANÇOISE *with envelope.* MARCEL *on bed staring at her.*

FRANÇOISE

How can you expect me to pester your mother when she's at dinner? Mmmnn? With Monsieur Swann sitting at the table. They say he's an intimate acquaintance of the President of the Republic himself, not to mention the Prefect of Police and the Prince of Wales of England. His coachman told me he dines with princesses. At least, that's what they call them. Still, that's what they say.

MARCEL *stares at her.*

8

FRANÇOISE

Anyway, they're still eating their ices. Perhaps I can give it to your mother with the coffee. I'll see. (*She turns the letter in her hands, peers at it.*) I can't believe it can be so important. What's so important about it?

41. *C.U. MARCEL, LOOKING AT HER.*

42. *EXT. THE GARDEN.*

>   *The table. The letter unopened under* MOTHER's *coffee cup.*

SWANN

When do you go back to Paris?

FATHER

In two weeks' time, I'm afraid.

SWANN

Yes, we shall be leaving shortly.

MOTHER

It's always so sad when the summer is over, and we have to leave Combray.

GRANDMOTHER

It's so much healthier here than Paris for Marcel, so much better for him.

SWANN

How is he?

FATHER (*tapping chest*)

Chest. Have to keep our eye on it.

>   SWANN *observes* MARCEL *peering down, half hidden, at his window. Their eyes meet.* SWANN *turns to the family.*

SWANN

I have a book I think Marcel might enjoy. I'll send it round tomorrow.

GRANDMOTHER
How very kind.

FATHER
We were talking about Monsieur Vinteuil before you came. Do you know him?

SWANN
We've never really met, no. But I've often wondered if he's any relation to the composer.

FATHER
Composer?

MOTHER
You must know the Vinteuil sonata!

FATHER
Do I?

SWANN
Don't you know it? It's an enchanting piece of work. I first heard it . . . oh, many years ago.

FATHER
Oh, the Vinteuil *sonata*? Yes, yes, of course, of course. Delightful.

SWANN
I wonder if this fellow's any relation. I must find out.

FATHER
I shouldn't think so.

The envelope remains unopened.

43. *THE GARDEN GATE CLOSES.*
The bell shudders.

44. *INT. MARCEL'S ROOM.*

MARCEL *is looking down from the window at* FATHER *and* MOTHER *alone at the table.*

MOTHER
He didn't look too well, I thought.

FATHER

It's his wife. To have thrown his life away for a woman like that. It's beyond me. He could have had any woman he liked. Did, in fact. Are you ready for bed?

MOTHER

You might at least let me ask after his daughter. He's so proud of her.

FATHER

Once you start asking after the daughter you'll end up asking after the wife. And then you'll find she'll be paying you calls. And there can be no question of that.

45. *INT. COMBRAY HOUSE. LANDING. STAIRS.*

> MARCEL *stands in the shadows.*
> *A faint glimmer of light from his parents' room.*
> *A flickering candle ascends the stairs. His* MOTHER *reaches the landing and sees* MARCEL.
> *He rushes to her, clasps her.*

MOTHER

What on earth are you doing?

> *He tries to pull her towards his door.*
> *She stops him.*

MOTHER (*whispering*)

No. Go back to your room. Do you want your father to catch you behaving like this?

> *Candlelight appears from end of corridor.*
> FATHER *emerges from his room.*

FATHER

What's this?

MOTHER

He wants me to kiss him good-night, in his room. He's behaving very stupidly.

> *Pause.*

FATHER

Go with him then.

11

MOTHER

Oh really, we mustn't indulge him.

FATHER

Rubbish. There's no need to make him ill. Sleep in his room just this once. (*Yawns.*) I'm off to bed anyway. Good night.

46. INT. MARCEL'S BEDROOM.

MARCEL *in bed, sobbing, clutching his* MOTHER'*s hand.*
She sits on the bed.

MOTHER (*gently*)

You must stop it. You'll make me cry in a minute, if you don't. (*Strokes him.*) There. There.

47. MOTHER'S EYES.

48. INT. MARCEL'S BEDROOM. LATER.

MOTHER *asleep in the other bed.*
MARCEL *turns in his bed, looks across to her.*

49. C.U. MARCEL.

50. INT. THE OPERA. PARIS. LATE 1898.

The audience are taking their seats.
MARCEL (19) *is seated in the orchestra stalls. Most people in the stalls are looking up at the boxes. The boxes are shadowy. Shafts of light flash as the doors to the boxes open. The entering figures stay in the shadows, then emerge into the light, the ladies with bare shoulders, pearls on their throats, unfurling their fans.*

Camera, in long shot, concentrates on one box; that of the PRINCESSE DE GUERMANTES, *an extremely beautiful woman of thirty-seven. With her is the* PRINCE DE GUERMANTES, *a man of fifty-two.*

Marcel *stares up. A voice whispers behind him:*
"That's the Prince and Princess."

The Princesse *sits on a coral sofa, by a mirror. She
wears a net of shells and pearls on her head, with a
necklace to match, and a bird of paradise headdress
curves round her face. She offers crystallized fruit to
a stout man.*

The box door opens. Enter the Duc *(52) and*
Duchesse de Guermantes *(40).*

Marcel's *eyes tighten. Voice: "Who's that?" Other
voice: "The Duchess. Her cousin." "And the man?"
"The Duke, you idiot."*

The Duc, *a magnificent figure, with monocle and
white carnation, drops his hand vertically upon the
shoulders of those in the box who are standing for
him and his wife. He bows to the* Princesse. *The*
Princesse *and* Duchesse *greet each other. The*
Duchesse *is in white muslin, carries a swansdown
fan, wears in her hair a simple aigrette. The* Duchesse *and* Princesse *appraise each other, laughing.*

The Duchesse *looks down into the stalls.*

Marcel *is watching her, compelling her to see him.
She suddenly does. She raises her white-gloved hand
and waves.*

The Princesse *turns to look down herself.
The* Duchesse *smiles down.*

51. *C.U. MARCEL, MUCH AFFECTED.*

Father *(V.O.)*

Today we'll walk the Guermantes' way.

52. *EXT. THE RIVER VIVONNE. COMBRAY. DAY.*
1893.

*Water lilies on the water.
Boys lowering glass jars to catch minnows.*

Marcel *(13) and family walking along the bank.*

13

FATHER

No, no, of course we can't get as far as the château. It's
much too far.

MOTHER (*to* MARCEL, *gently*)

But you'll be able to see the Duchess on Sunday. She's
coming to Combray for the wedding.

GRANDMOTHER

I thing Marcel's fascinated by the name as much as
anything else. Aren't you?

FATHER

The name stands for something. They're one of the
oldest and noblest families in France.

GRANDMOTHER

Yes, but I meant the actual sound. It's golden.
Guermantes.

53. *INT. MARCEL'S ROOM. NIGHT. 1888.*

> MARCEL (8) *alone with a magic lantern.*
> *The image of Geneviève de Brabant (ancestress of
> the Guermantes family) floats over the walls and
> ceiling.*

MARCEL (*V.O., murmuring*)

Guermantes.

54. *INT. SAINT-HILAIRE CHURCH, COMBRAY. 1893.*

> *Chapel of Gilbert the Bad.*
> *Camera pans down stained-glass window.*
> *The wedding in progress. White hawthorn blossoms
> over the altar.*

55. *INT. CHURCH. CONGREGATION.*

> *The* DUCHESSE DE GUERMANTES (35) *seen from* MAR-
> CEL'S *point of view.*

56. C.U. MARCEL.

> *Looking at her.*

57. C.U. THE DUCHESSE.

> *She turns her head, a slight smile on her lips.*

58. THE CHÂTEAU OF GUERMANTES (IDEALIZED IMAGE).

> *Long shot across the lake to the château.*
> *In the far distance the figures of the DUCHESSE and MARCEL, walking slowly by the lake. She is holding his hand.*
> *A woman's voice (not the DUCHESSE's) heard over:*

> VOICE

You are a poet. I can tell. Tell me about your poems. Tell me about the poems you intend to write.

59. EXT. GARDEN. COMBRAY. DAY. 1893. LONG SHOT.

> *SWANN (45) and MARCEL (13) are sitting together in the garden. Their heads are close.*
> *SWANN is riffling through the pages of a book.*
> *Smiling, he reads a sentence or two to MARCEL.*
> *MARCEL's reaction is animated. He takes the book from SWANN, and studies the page.*

> *Chimes of the church bell.*
> *Bird sounds.*

60. EXT. GARDEN. COMBRAY. SUNSET.

> *MARCEL sitting in a hooded wicker chair, reading. He is alone in the garden.*

> *Chimes of the church bell.*

> *FRANÇOISE with a carving knife suddenly emerges from kitchen chasing a chicken.*
> *MARCEL looks up startled.*

15

FRANÇOISE (*savagely*)

Come here! Come here!

> FRANÇOISE *chases the chicken into the kitchen.*
> *Shouts of "Come here!" The chicken's squawks*
> *cease.*
>
> MARCEL'S *hands clench.*

61. INT. COMBRAY HOUSE. LAVATORY.

> MARCEL *at window stares down at the streets of*
> *Combray, silent, still, in the heat.*
> *The church steeple.*
>
> *A young girl, alone, crosses a street, disappears.*
>
> *Flowering currant cascades through the window.*

62. MARCEL'S EYES.

> *A sigh, offscreen, is heard from* MARCEL.
>
> *The camera slowly leaves him and rests on the*
> *flowering currant, and the view.*

63. EXT. M. VINTEUIL'S HOUSE. MONTJOUVAIN.
DAY.

> *In foreground* MARCEL *and family.* M. VINTEUIL *(60)*
> *comes quickly from the front door and walks towards*
> *them.*
>
> *Through the drawing room window* MLLE. VINTEUIL
> *(18) and her* FRIEND *(21) can be clearly seen playing*
> *a duet.*

M. VINTEUIL

How very nice to see you. Good afternoon to you all.
(*He glances back to the window.*) Yes, as you see, the
two young ladies are practicing away. My daughter's
friend is really quite talented. I hope my daughter will
benefit from her example, her enthusiasm. I'm too old
now, too old to teach, but my daughter's friend is so
able, so charming, so able.

The camera focuses on Mlle. Vinteuil *and her* Friend, *playing. They do not look out of the window.*

64. *INT. RAILWAY CARRIAGE. LITTLE TRAIN FROM LA RASPELIERE. 1901. NIGHT.*

Marcel *(21) and* Albertine *(21).* Albertine *is in the middle of speaking.*

ALBERTINE

I know Vinteuil's daughter almost as well as I know her friend. I always call them my two big sisters.

65. *EXT. SWANN'S HOUSE. TANSONVILLE. 1893.*

The path by the side of Swann's *park.*
A hedge of white and pink hawthorns.

Marcel *(13) comes into shot. He stands looking at the hawthorns.*

FATHER (V.O.)

Today we'll walk Swann's way.

66. *FARTHER ALONG THE PATH.*

Mother *and* Father *walking ahead.* Marcel *straggles after. Suddenly he stops.*

67. *GAP IN HEDGE.*

Through gap in hedge he sees a pond. A fishing line rests by the side of the pond, its float bobbing in the water. By the side of the road a straw bucket.
Along a gravel path a watering pipe is coiled, water emerging from the holes along its length like a fan over the flowers—jasmine, pansies, verbenas, wall flowers.

Suddenly his head jolts. A girl with black eyes, holding a trowel, is looking at him. It is Gilberte. *She is thirteen.*

17

68. EXT. PARK AT TANSONVILLE. LONG SHOT.

>   MARCEL *at hedge.* MOTHER *and* FATHER *continuing up the hill.*

69. THE HEDGE.

>   *He stares at her.*
>   *She looks at him with a half smile, a curious intensity.*

70. C.U. GILBERTE'S FACE.

>   *Her black eyes, smiling.*

71. C.U. MARCEL.

>   *His face, bcwildered, even alarmed.*

72. GILBERTE'S EYES.

>   ODETTE (V.O.)
>   Gilberte, come along. What are you doing?

73. THE HEDGE.

>   ODETTE *(Mme. Swann) dressed in white, comes into view. She is thirty-six.*
>   *She is followed by the* BARON DE CHARLUS, *wearing a white linen suit. He is forty-six.*
>   GILBERTE *turns to them. They regard* MARCEL *for a moment, and then continue walking.*

74. FARTHER ALONG THE PATH.

>   MOTHER *and* FATHER *have stopped and turned.*
>   ODETTE, CHARLUS, *and* GILBERTE *glimpsed by them moving through trees.*

>   MOTHER
>   I thought she was in Paris.

FATHER

She's sent Swann to Paris alone, that's what she's done, so that she can be alone with Charlus. That was the Baron de Charlus. I recognized him.

MOTHER

Who is he?

FATHER

Her newest lover. Or her oldest, I don't know. I take no interest in these matters. It's intolerable. And in front of the girl too.

> *He calls to* MARCEL, *who has not moved. "Marcel! Come on!"*

MOTHER

I don't think Swann cares any more. I honestly think he's quite indifferent.

75. *C.U. ODETTE, SEEN THROUGH LEAVES.*

76. *C.U. ODETTE, FOURTEEN YEARS YOUNGER.*

77. *INT. THE VERDURINS' HOUSE, PARIS. 1879.*

> *Over* ODETTE's *face, the voice of* MME. VERDURIN.

MME. VERDURIN (V.O.)

She's just a little tiny piece of perfection. Aren't you? Look! She's blushing!

ODETTE (*demurely*)

Oh, Madame Verdurin.

78. *TWO SHOT: SWANN (31) AND M. VERDURIN (39).*

> SWANN *is looking towards* ODETTE. *He turns from her as* M. VERDURIN *speaks.*

M. VERDURIN

I'm going to light my pipe. Do light a pipe if you wish. There's no ceremony here.

MME. VERDURIN (V.O.)

No ceremony, no snobbery, no airs, and no graces.

SWANN *looks, slightly uneasily, towards* MME.
VERDURIN.

MME. VERDURIN (V.O.)

We're real people here, I hope, not stuffed dummies.
That's the kind of house you find yourself in, Monsieur
Swann. And we're delighted to welcome you.

SWANN

You're very kind.

M. VERDURIN

Ah! Dechambre's ready to play. A really original piece
we've discovered. A sonata by a man called Vinteuil.

79. THE ROOM.

MME. VERDURIN (37) *is sitting in a high Swedish
chair of waxed pinewood. About the room are* DR.
COTTARD (35), MME. COTTARD (31), BRICHOT (42),
and DECHAMBRE (20).

MME. VERDURIN

No, no, no, not my sonata! I shall have to stay in bed for
a week. Oh well, I'll have to surrender to it, I suppose.
Make myself ill for the sake of art. Monsieur Swann,
you're not comfortable—sit by Mademoiselle de Crécy
on the sofa. You can make room for him, Odette, can't
you, you exquisite little thing?

ODETTE

Oh yes, Madame Verdurin, I think so.

SWANN *sits next to* ODETTE. *She lowers her lashes.*

80. LONG SHOT OF ROOM.

DECHAMBRE *plays on the piano the section of the
sonata which includes the "little phrase."*
MME. VERDURIN *sits with her eyes tight shut, her
hands to her face.*

81. *SWANN AND ODETTE.*

> Swann *listens intently, frowning.*

82. *INT. ODETTE'S HOUSE IN RUE LAPÉROUSE.*
    PARIS. 1879.

> *In the lobby leading to the drawing room a long box filled with chrysanthemums. Palm trees growing out of pots of Chinese porcelain, lamps in porcelain vases, screens upon which are fastened photographs. Fans, bows of ribbon, large cushions of Japanese silk, a dromedary of inlaid silver work and a toad carved in jade on the mantelpiece, a portrait of Odette upon an easel.*

> Odette's *arms and neck are bare. She wears a wrapper of mauve crepe de Chine. She is playing the "little phrase" on the piano, badly.* Swann *looks down at her, listening.*

Swann

Play it again.

Odette (laughing)

Again! The little phrase, that's all.

> *She plays.*

Odette

I play so badly.

> *He kisses her neck, throat, mouth, as she falteringly plays. She stops.*

Odette

Now make up your mind. Do you want me to play the phrase or do you want to play with me?

Swann

That music belongs to us. It's our anthem. (*Kissing her.*) Don't you think it's beautiful?

Odette

It's very nice.

21

SWANN

There's a painting by Botticelli. Jethro's daughter. It's you. She is you.

ODETTE (*kissing him quickly*)

You are sweet.

83. *INT. ODETTE'S HOUSE. EARLY EVENING. 1880.*

> SWANN *is sitting uncomfortably on a sofa as* ODETTE *fusses about him, arranging cushions around him. She moves a tray of tea on a side table nearer to him. She places his feet on a footstool and settles further cushions about him, giggling.*
>
> SWANN *takes from his pocket a fat wad of banknotes. He gives it to her.*

SWANN

You said you needed some money.

ODETTE

Oh darling!

> *She bends to kiss him.*

84. *ODETTE FROM SWANN'S P.O.V.*

> *She bends to kiss him.*
>
> *Her cheeks, smooth and flushed, come closer to his eye and show a coarser grain.*

85. *OVER ODETTE TO SWANN.*

> *She is kissing him.*
>
> *His eyes are open.*

86. *EXT. ODETTE'S HOUSE. NIGHT.*

> *A carriage draws up.* SWANN *gets out, goes to door, knocks.*
> *Silence.*
> ODETTE *in negligee. She stares at him.*

SWANN

It's late I know. I'm sorry.

ODETTE

But you weren't coming tonight.
What happened to your banquet?

SWANN

I left early. To see you.

ODETTE

But I'm asleep. I have a terrible headache. I was asleep.

SWANN

Let me come in. I'll . . . soothe you.

ODETTE

You say you're not coming, I don't feel well, I go to bed,
and then you arrive, in the middle of the night.

SWANN

It's only eleven o'clock.

ODETTE

It's the middle of the night for me. (*Softer.*) Please. Not
now. Tomorrow. Tomorrow night. I'll be better. It will
be sweet. Think of that.

87. *EXT. SWANN'S HOUSE. PARIS. NIGHT.*

> *The carriage draws up.* COACHMAN *opens carriage
> door.* SWANN *does not move.*

SWANN

Go back. To rue Lapérouse.

88. *EXT. RUE LAPÉROUSE. NIGHT.*

> *The lamps in the street are now out. The street is
> quite dark but for one light in one house, shining
> through the slats of the shutters.*
>
> SWANN *walks quietly to this window and listens
> outside it.*
>
> *Murmurs of a man's voice.*

23

He stands, pained, uncertain.

He suddenly knocks on the shutters.
Silence.

He knocks again.

A man's voice: "Who's that?"

As the window and shutters are being opened SWANN
speaks.

SWANN

Just happened to be passing. Wanted to know if you
were feeling better.

The shutters open.

An OLD GENTLEMAN *holding a lamp stares at him. In
the background of a quite unfamiliar room stands*
ANOTHER OLD GENTLEMAN.

SWANN

I'm terribly sorry. I'm afraid I have the wrong house.

GENTLEMAN

Good night, sir.

He closes the shutters.

SWANN, *in the dark, looks towards* ODETTE's *house,
which is dark and silent.*

89. INT. ODETTE'S BEDROOM.

ODETTE *is combing her hair at her dressing table.*

SWANN

Odette, I must ask you a few questions.

ODETTE

What now?

She looks at him.

ODETTE

Nasty ones, I'm sure.

SWANN

Since you have known me have you . . . known any other
men?

ODETTE

I knew it was that kind of question from your face. No. I have not. Why would I want other men, you silly? I have you.

Pause.

SWANN

What about women?

ODETTE

Women?

SWANN

You remember once Madame Verdurin said to you: "I know how to melt you, all right. You're not made of marble."

ODETTE

You asked me about that ages ago.

SWANN

I know—

ODETTE

I told you it was a joke. A joke, that's all.

SWANN

Have you ever, with her?

ODETTE

I've told you, no! You know quite well. Anyway, she's not like that.

SWANN

Don't say "You know quite well." Say "I have never done anything of that sort with Madame Verdurin or with any other woman."

ODETTE (automatically)

I have never done anything of that sort with Madame Verdurin or with any other woman.

Silence.

SWANN

Can you swear to me on the medal round your neck?

25

ODETTE

Oh, you make me sick! What's the matter with you today?

SWANN

Tell me, on your medal, yes or no, whether you have ever done those things?

ODETTE

How do I know? I don't even know what you mean. What things? Perhaps I have, years ago, when I didn't know what I was doing. Perhaps two or three times, I don't know.

Pause.

SWANN

How many times exactly?

ODETTE

For God's sake! (*Slight pause.*) Anyway it's all so long ago. I've never given it a thought. Anyone would think you're trying to put ideas into my head—just to get me to do it again.

SWANN

It's quite a simple question. And you must remember. You must remember with whom . . . my love. The last time, for instance.

ODETTE *relaxes, speaks lightly.*

ODETTE

Oh, I don't know. I think in the Bois . . . on the island . . . one evening . . . you were dining with those Guermantes. At the next table was a woman I hadn't seen for ages. She said to me, "Come round behind the rock there and look at the moonlight on the water." At first I just yawned and said, "No, I'm too tired." But she swore there'd never been any moonlight to touch it. "I've heard that tale before," I said to her. I knew quite well what she was after.

26

90. *EXT. SWANN'S PARK AND HOUSE AT TANSON-VILLE. DAY.*

>*No one in sight.*

>>SWANN (*V.O., with fatigue*)
>Perhaps two or three times.

>*Bird song.*
>I knew quite well what she was after.

91. *EXT. M. VINTEUIL'S HOUSE AT MONTJOUVAIN. EARLY EVENING. 1895.*

>*The camera, still, looking into the drawing room window.*

>*MLLE. VINTEUIL enters, stands, goes to mantelpiece, takes photograph, walks to sofa, places photo on table by sofa, lies down on sofa.*

>*Her FRIEND enters. MLLE. VINTEUIL sits up, makes room on sofa. FRIEND looks at her in silence.*
>*MLLE. VINTEUIL lies down again, yawns.*

>>FRIEND
>I wish you'd change that ghastly dress. Are you going to mourn your father forever?

>*MLLE. VINTEUIL rises, walks to window to close shutters.*

>>FRIEND
>Leave them open. I'm hot.

>>MLLE. VINTEUIL
>But people can see us.

>*FRIEND smiles.*

>>MLLE. VINTEUIL
>I mean see us reading, or whatever we're doing.

>>FRIEND
>And what if they do see us reading? Who could object to that?

>*Pause.*

27

Where's your book?

MLLE. VINTEUIL

What book?

FRIEND

How can you read without a book, you stupid slut?
Anyway, I'm not reading, I'm thinking.

MLLE. VINTEUIL

What about?

> *The* FRIEND *walks towards* MLLE. VINTEUIL. *She
> kisses her.*
>
> MLLE. VINTEUIL *breaks away.* FRIEND *chases her.*
>
> MLLE. VINTEUIL *falls on sofa.* FRIEND *lies on top of
> her.*

MLLE. VINTEUIL

My father's looking at us. Stop.

> FRIEND *turns, picks up the photograph.*

FRIEND

Do you know what I'm going to do to your dear dead
father?

> *She whispers.*

MLLE. VINTEUIL

You wouldn't.

FRIEND

Oh yes I would. Oh yes I will.

> MLLE. VINTEUIL *runs to the window and closes the
> shutters.*
>
> *Camera turns slowly away from the window.*
>
> MARCEL *(15), watching.*

92. *EXT. COUNTRY ROAD NEAR COMBRAY. SUN-
SET. 1895.*

> *Long shot.* DR. PERCEPIED's *carriage driving fast.*

He passes MARCEL *and family walking, stops.*
He invites the family into the carriage. They climb in.
MARCEL *sits with the coachman.*

93. MARCEL'S P.O.V. FROM MOVING CARRIAGE.

The twin steeples of Martinville church and, in the distance, a third steeple from another village.

At first the distance between the Martinville steeples and the other is clear, definite. But as the road winds and in the sun's reflection they seem to change position. The third, although rising from higher ground in the distance, suddenly appears to be standing by their side, to be one of them.

Further views of them, as the carriage progresses:

Only the Martinville steeples seen; the third not in sight.

The third very dim, quivering.

The Martinville steeples almost blotted out; the third startlingly clear, luminous.

The three steeples apparently side by side, dancing together in the last rays of the sun.

94. C.U. MARCEL'S FACE, ALIVE.

95. EXT. ALLÉE DES ACACIAS. PARIS. WINTER. 1897. DAY.

MARCEL (17) *watches a victoria approach.*
ODETTE *lies back in it, holding a violet parasol.*

TWO MEN, *near* MARCEL, *doff their hats, bow.*
She smiles, gently, at them.

96. ODETTE'S EYES.

97. *THE VICTORIA PASSES.*

> *The* TWO MEN *look at each other.*

> FIRST MAN
>
> I was in bed with her the afternoon General MacMahon resigned.

98. *EXT. CHAMPS-ÉLYSÉES GARDENS. PARIS. 1897.*

> GILBERTE (17) *whispering with girl friends in the bushes. A girl's voice laughing, "Oh Gilberte!"*

99. *MARCEL WATCHING GILBERTE.*

100. *SWANN IN FOREGROUND STANDING BY A TREE, WATCHING MARCEL WATCH GILBERTE.*

> MARCEL *is unaware of* SWANN's *presence.*

101. *EXT. SWANN'S HOUSE. PARIS.*

> GILBERTE *running towards the house and entering.*

102. *EXT. MARCEL'S HOUSE. BOULEVARD MALSHERBES. PARIS. EVENING.*

> MARCEL *entering the house.*

103. *INT. MARCEL'S HOUSE. THE HALL. 1897.*

> MARCEL (17) *passes the open door of his* FATHER's *study.*

> FATHER
>
> Ah Marcel. Come here.

> MARCEL *goes into the study.*

104. *INT. STUDY.*

> FATHER
>
> Let me introduce you to His Excellency the Ambassador, the Marquis de Norpois.

They bow.
The Marquis de Norpois *is seventy.*

Marcel

Good evening, sir.

Norpois

Good evening. Your father tells me you wish to pursue writing, as a career?

Marcel

I . . . yes, sir. I think so, sir.

Norpois

Rather than diplomacy?

Marcel

I . . . think so, sir.

Norpois

You are not inclined to follow in the distinguished footsteps of your father?

Father

Marcel is not yet at the age, of course, where he need take a final decision.

Norpois

A career in writing can bear surprisingly rewarding fruits, if I may say so, if, that is, one maintains the proper balance of industry, determination, and ambition, allied to a clearly defined understanding of one's own limitations and capabilities, and if one possesses, of course (*with a smile*), talent. The son of a friend of mine, for example—two years ago he published a study dealing with "The Sense of the Infinite on the Western Shore of Lake Victoria Nyanza," and followed it last spring with a remarkably cutting treatise on "The Use of the Repeating Rifle in the Bulgarian Army"—written from an entirely different standpoint, of course. He is now, I would say, in a class by himself. I happen to know that his name has been mentioned, and not at all unfavorably, as a possible candidate for the Academy of Moral Sciences.

31

FATHER

Really?

NORPOIS

Oh yes. I am glad to say that success, usually reserved for agitators and mischief-makers, has certainly crowned his efforts. (*To* MARCEL.) What have you written?

MARCEL

Sir?

NORPOIS

What have you written?

MARCEL

Nothing . . . I'm afraid . . . that is actually finished.

FATHER *takes a piece of paper from desk.*

FATHER

What about this?

MARCEL

What?

FATHER

Your piece. Your prose poem, as you called it. Your piece about steeples.

MARCEL (*startled*)

Oh no! No . . . that's . . .

FATHER

It's finished, isn't it?

MARCEL

Yes, but it was written years ago. It's . . . juvenile.

NORPOIS

One can often discern a great deal from early efforts. (*To* FATHER.) May I?

FATHER (*passing paper*)

Please. Please.

NORPOIS (*glancing at it, murmuring*)

Steeples.

M. Norpois *reads. Silence.* M. Norpois *finishes reading, looks up, clears his throat, hands paper back to* Marcel, *staring at him.*
Father *takes paper, puts it back in desk.*

FATHER

Shall we go in to dinner?

105. INT. DINING ROOM.

The family and Norpois *at dinner, with* Grand-mother.

NORPOIS

You have a chef of the first order, madame. That was a positive banquet. How rarely does one eat a boeuf en daube in which the jelly does not tast like glue and the beef has caught the flavor of the carrots. Admirable!

MOTHER

I am so pleased.

FATHER

Were you at the Foreign Ministry dinner last night? I couldn't go.

NORPOIS

No. I must confess I renounced it for a party of a very different sort. I was dining with the beautiful Madame Swann.

Mother *and* Father *start.* Marcel *looks at him keenly.*

MOTHER

How interesting. Were there many people there?

NORPOIS

Frankly, I would say it was a house which is especially attractive to gentlemen. There were several married men there, but their wives (*with a smile*) were all, as it happened, unwell.

MOTHER

And is Monsieur Swann . . . well, Your Excellency?

NORPOIS (winking)

Oh, he seems to be leading an active enough life by all accounts, as active as his wife, one gathers, from the way tongues wag.

FRANÇOISE *and* FOOTMAN *enter with a pudding.*

NORPOIS

A Nesselrode pudding! As well! I shall need a slimming course, madame.

He helps himself.

MARCEL

Was Madame Swann's daughter at the dinner?

NORPOIS

She was indeed. A charming young lady.

MARCEL

I wonder if you could possibly find an opportunity to introduce me to her.

MOTHER *and* FATHER *stare at him.*

NORPOIS *looks at him icily, digs into his pudding and mutters:*

NORPOIS

Of course, of course.

106. *EXT. CHAMPS-ÉLYSÉES GARDEN. DAY. (SAME AS SHOT NO. 100.)*

GILBERTE *whispering with girl friends in the bushes.*

MARCEL *watching.*

SWANN *absent.*

A girl's voice laughing, "Oh Gilberte!"

107. *EXT. SWANN'S HOUSE. PARIS. EVENING.*

GILBERTE *comes out of the house with a young man. They walk down the street and disappear.*

The camera finds MARCEL.
He looks after GILBERTE *for a moment, turns, and walks away.*

108. EXT. THE PROMENADE. BALBEC. DAY. 1898.

From outside the Grand Hotel the camera looks along the promenade and focuses, through the crowds, in the distance, on FIVE GIRLS, *strikingly dressed, quite distinct in their carriage, one pushing a bicycle, two carrying golf clubs.*

They approach slowly.
No sound.

109. INT. DINING ROOM. BALBEC HOTEL. DAY. 1898.

Very hot afternoon. The curtains are drawn, although not fully, to shield the room from the glare.

Through spaces between the curtains the sea flashes and in one of the spaces SAINT-LOUP (20), *dressed in an almost white, very thin suit, is seen striding from the beach towards the hotel, his monocle dropping from his eye and being replaced.*

The camera shifts to look through the foyer to the glass front of the hotel, the bottom half of which is filled with sea, SAINT-LOUP *in foreground striding towards a carriage and pair. He jumps onto the box seat and takes the reins from the groom. The hotel manager rushes out with a letter for him.* SAINT-LOUP *opens the letter and, starting the horses at the same time, drives off.*

No sound.

110. EXT. PROMENADE. BALBEC. DAY. 1898.

Close Shot.
The BARON DE CHARLUS (51) *stands in front of a*

playbill. Dark suit, dark moustache. His eyes stare piercingly at something.

No sound.

111. INT. COMPARTMENT OF MOVING TRAIN. DAY.
1898:

        MARCEL *(18) and* GRANDMOTHER *(66).*

                  MARCEL

I really don't see why I couldn't have gone to Venice.

            GRANDMOTHER *(gently)*

The doctor said the air at Balbec would be better for you, you know that.

        MARCEL *grunts.*

                  MARCEL

I need a drink.

        She looks at him.

                  MARCEL

You know I'm ill! Do you want me to have another choking fit? The doctor *ordered* me to have some brandy as soon as the journey started. Anyway, I feel ill now. I *need* some brandy.

                GRANDMOTHER

Well, go and have some, then.

                  MARCEL

It's necessary for my health.

112. INT. COMPARTMENT. DAY.

        GRANDMOTHER *alone, reading.* MARCEL *enters, drunk.*

                  MARCEL

Charming waiters. Excellent service. Even the ticket collector was a man of . . . great refinement. Witty too.

        He staggers.

                  MARCEL

To be honest . . . to be honest, I thought I would miss

Mama in Balbec, but now I know I won't. No. The doctor was absolutely right about the brandy. Absolutely. I feel very much better.

He sits suddenly, looks at GRANDMOTHER.

MARCEL

By the way, did you want anything?

GRANDMOTHER

No, no. Why don't you try to get a little sleep?

He closes his eyes.

113. *MARCEL'S BLURRED P.O.V.*

GRANDMOTHER *looking at him under her veil.*

114. *INT. MARCEL'S BEDROOM, GRAND HOTEL. BALBEC. NIGHT. 1898.*

MARCEL *sits on the bed, looking desolately about the room, which is curtained and shuttered. A clock ticks heavily. He looks along a row of bookcases with glass fronts, which glint in the light, and stares at a long mirror which stands in a corner. He is reflected in it.*

He cranes his neck to look up at the high ceilings, shivers, sees again his reflection in the mirror. He goes to the mirror and turns its face to the corner.

He goes to the wall, hesitates, and then knocks tentatively three times.

A pause, and then three authoritative knocks sound from the next room.

He sits on the bed. The door opens. GRANDMOTHER *comes in, dressed in a loose cambric gown.*

GRANDMOTHER

Are you ill?

MARCEL

No. Just tired.

She goes to him, leans over him, touches his forehead.

He embraces her fiercely, kissing her cheek.
She holds him.

GRANDMOTHER

Now stand up. (*He does.*) And let's get these boots off.

MARCEL

No, no, I'll . . .

GRANDMOTHER

No, no, I'll do it. It's easy for me to do it. Just put your
hand on my shoulder and we'll get these boots off.

Kneeling, she unbuttons his boots, while he looks
down at her gravely.

115. INT. BEDROOM. MORNING.

Sea and sky flashing in glass fronts of bookcases.

An opened trunk, with clothes strewn about it, is on
the floor.

MARCEL, with wet face, naked to the waist, moves
from wash basin to towel rack, picks up a clean
starched towel, which crackles, wipes his face, look-
ing out of the window.

Dazzling sea from window.

He slowly puts towel back on the rack, gazing out to
the sea.

His face, happy.

116. INT. BEDROOM. MORNING.

FRANÇOISE stands, looking down at the trunk.
She clicks her teeth, begins to fold clothes and put
them into drawers.

117. INT. HOTEL DINING ROOM. LUNCH.

MARCEL and GRANDMOTHER are sitting at a table by
the windows, which are closed.
GRANDMOTHER leans over to a side window and
opens it. A gust of wind blows in. Newspapers and

menus scatter. Ladies clasp their hats, veils fly up.
Remonstrances from other guests. Waiters rush to
close window.

MARCEL *looks at* GRANDMOTHER.

In background, at dining room door, an OLD LADY
(66) appears.
She sees GRANDMOTHER *and her face brightens.*
GRANDMOTHER, *however, lowers her eyes, does not*
respond.
The OLD LADY *looks away, is escorted to her table.*

MARCEL

That lady seemed to know you.

GRANDMOTHER

Yes, she does. She's the Marquise de Villeparisis.

MARCEL (staring at GRANDMOTHER)

But she's one of your closest friends! Aren't you going to
speak to her?

GRANDMOTHER

One does not go to the seaside to meet people, however
pleasant. One goes to the seaside for peace, relaxation,
and fresh air. Madame de Villeparisis understands that
perfectly.

118.   *EXT. THE PROMENADE. DAY.*

MARCEL *stands alone.*
In the distance, he sees FIVE GIRLS, *slowly approach-*
ing through the crowds. One pushes a bicycle, two
carry golf clubs.
He stares at them.
A call: "Marcel!" He turns. GRANDMOTHER *ap-*
proaches with MME. DE VILLEPARISIS.

GRANDMOTHER

Let me introduce my grandson. Marcel—the Marquise
de Villeparisis.

He bows.

How do you do? Your grandmother and I have just collided in a shop doorway. I had no idea she was in Balbec. A delightful surprise.

GRANDMOTHER

You are expecting your nephew to join you from Paris, you say?

MME. DE VILLEPARISIS

I am expecting two nephews. To be exact, one nephew and one great-nephew. One is the uncle of the other (*she chuckles*), but I am the aunt of them both.

The two ladies walk on together.

MARCEL follows them, but suddenly pauses and looks back along the promenade.

No sign of the girls.

119.   INT. DINING ROOM. AFTERNOON.

The curtains are drawn. MARCEL sits alone with coffee. From his position he can see through the foyer to the glass front of the hotel.

Against a background of sea, SAINT-LOUP strides towards a carriage and pair, jumps on the box seat, takes an envelope from the hotel manager, opens it, starts the horses, drives off.

120.   C.U. BARON DE CHARLUS IN FRONT OF PLAY-BILL.

121.   EXT. THE PROMENADE. DAY.

MARCEL, feeling he is being watched, turns.

From his P.O.V. sees CHARLUS in front of the playbill. He wears a dark suit, and slaps the leg of his trousers with a switch, staring at MARCEL.

He turns away abruptly to examine the playbill, takes out a notebook, makes a note, looks at his watch, *pulls his straw hat over his eyes, looks up and down the front, sighs, walks quickly away.*

MARCEL *stares after him.*

122.   EXT. PROMENADE. DAY.

The little band of GIRLS *walking along the front. They keep to an absolutely straight, remorseless course, appearing not to see those in their path. Some people make way for them automatically, some with a slight panic. The* GIRLS *ignore them and proceed with an arrogant assurance, occasionally jumping over an obstacle.*

One of the GIRLS *suddenly springs onto the platform of the bandstand and jumps over an old man, sitting underneath it in a deck chair. His cap is brushed by her feet. He looks up, terrified. The* GIRLS *laugh and applaud.*

They draw closer. The sun is bright on the sea.

They are seen against the sea.

A confusion of faces, eyes, colors, hair, moving together, as parts of one unit.

Suddenly one girl's face is precisely focused.
She is dark, wears a polo cap, pushes a bicycle.
She turns her head, looks into the camera.
ALBERTINE. *She is eighteen.*

123.   EXT. PROMENADE.

MARCEL.
The GIRLS *passing.*

ALBERTINE *looking at him.*
She turns away from him.

124.   INT. FOYER. HOTEL.

MME. DE VILLEPARISIS.   CHARLUS.   SAINT-LOUP.
MARCEL.

41

M<small>ME</small>. <small>DE</small> V<small>ILLEPARISIS</small>

The Baron de Charlus.

> C<small>HARLUS</small>, *without looking at* M<small>ARCEL</small>, *extends his suede-gloved hand, crooks his little finger, forefinger, and thumb, leaving his middle two fingers extended.* M<small>ARCEL</small> *takes them.*

M<small>ME DE</small> V<small>ILLEPARISIS</small>

The Marquis de Saint-Loup-en-Bray.

> S<small>AINT</small>-L<small>OUP</small>'s *face and body are immobile, his eyes expressionless. He extends his arm abruptly, at full length.* M<small>ARCEL</small> *takes his hand.*

125. RIVEBELLE RESTAURANT, NEAR BALBEC. EVENING.

> *Rivebelle Restaurant possesses a large garden, with tables.*
>
> *Inside the restaurant a gypsy band plays. All the tables are taken and waiters are moving very quickly in all directions, some arguing with head waiters who respond by prodding them in the ribs on their way. Vast counters of hors d'oeuvres. Two very fat lady cashiers sit behind a bank of flowers.*
>
> S<small>AINT</small>-L<small>OUP</small> *and* M<small>ARCEL</small> *are at the door with a waiter, who takes* M<small>ARCEL</small>'s *coat.*

S<small>AINT</small>-L<small>OUP</small>

Perhaps you should keep your coat. It's rather draughty in here.

M<small>ARCEL</small>

No, no. Not at all.

> *They pass into the restaurant and move through the crowded tables. Women look up as they pass.* S<small>AINT</small>-L<small>OUP</small> *bows once or twice.*
>
> *One* W<small>OMAN</small> *turns to another and whispers:*

42

WOMAN

He remembered me!

> SAINT-LOUP *and* MARCEL *sit down and are given menus and beer.*

126. *EXT. RIVEBELLE. THE GARDEN.*

> *Night has not quite fallen. The lamps in the restaurant cause a pale green reflection in the windows.*
> *Impression of an aquarium.*

127. *INT. RESTAURANT.*

SAINT-LOUP

It isn't very often I meet anyone who's interested in writing, who wants to write, who's concerned about the expression of experience through words.

> SAINT-LOUP *waits for* MARCEL *to respond.* MARCEL *does not.*

SAINT-LOUP

The world of "society," to which I unfortunately belong, displays nothing but a carefully cultivated ignorance which over the centuries has become banality of mind, masquerading behind gesture, behind manner, behind arrogance, as good breeding. It never occurs to them that their posture and pretensions have become atrophied. But in fact they know nothing and are interested in nothing except money and position. They're philistines.

> *The hors d'oeuvres are served.*
> *They eat.*

SAINT-LOUP

You looked at me critically, I thought, when I spoke to my groom this evening.

MARCEL

I thought you were a little harsh with him.

SAINT-LOUP

I regard him as my equal. Why should I go out of my way to speak politely to him? You seem to think I should treat him with respect, *as an inferior*. I treat him in the same way I treat my family. You're talking like an aristocrat!

They eat.

MARCEL

These places always make me think of an aquarium. You wonder when the people outside are going to break through the glass and devour the fish.

SAINT-LOUP *stares at him.*

128. *THE TABLE. LATER.*

They are drinking port.

SAINT-LOUP

My family disapproves of me violently because I'm in love with an actress. She's got more refinement and sensitivity in her little finger than they have in their whole body. However, the fact remains, quite frankly, that she's driving me mad. I dream about her, all the time. Last night I dreamt I was in a house. My sergeant major was the host. I was sitting with him drinking. Suddenly I heard sounds, her sounds . . . you know . . . her sounds. Someone was with her, in her room. I could hear her sounds. But my sergeant major would not allow me to go to her room. He refused absolutely. He was very angry, he said it would be most indiscreet of me, most impolite, most . . . ungentlemanly.

Pause.

SAINT-LOUP

What an idiotic dream.

SAINT-LOUP *is sweating.*

44

SAINT-LOUP

I won't be a moment.

> SAINT-LOUP *rises and forces his way through the packed tables to the door.*

> MARCEL *calls a* WAITER.

MARCEL

A piece of bread, please.

WAITER

Certainly, Monsieur le Baron.

MARCEL

I am not a baron.

WAITER

Sorry, Monsieur le Comte.

> SAINT-LOUP *appears at the door with* MARCEL's *coat. He looks swiftly at the packed tables and to where* MARCEL *is sitting at the far end of the red plush bench, which runs round the side of the room. He jumps onto the bench, and from the bench steps onto the narrow ledge which runs behind it.*

> *The staff, stopping their service in midtracks, and the other diners watch as* SAINT-LOUP *runs along the ledge, balancing himself with his arms, like a tightrope walker. Discreet applause breaks out. He arrives at his table, jumps down and hands* MARCEL *his coat.*

SAINT-LOUP

I thought it was becoming a little chilly.

129. *INT. MARCEL'S BEDROOM. HOTEL. NIGHT.*

> MARCEL *alone in the room. A knock at the door.*

MARCEL

Who is it?

CHARLUS

It is Charlus. May I come in?

MARCEL *opens the door.* CHARLUS *enters, a book in his hand.*

CHARLUS

My nephew was telling me that you were often depressed before going to bed, that you found difficulty in getting to sleep, and that you admired the work of Anatole France. I happen to have one of his novels with me. I thought you might like to read it, that it might relax you.

MARCEL

How very kind of you. Thank you. But you must think these ... moods of mine ... at night ... very stupid.

CHARLUS

No, why? You have not, perhaps, any personal merit. So few have. But for a time at least you have youth and that is always charming. You have also placed your affection wisely, in your grandmother. It is a legitimate affection, I mean one that is repaid. That's a rare enough state of affairs.

CHARLUS *walks up and down the room, thoughtfully.*

CHARLUS

I have another volume of Anatole France in my room. I will have it brought for you.

CHARLUS *does not move. They stand in silence.*

MARCEL

Please don't bother. One volume will be quite enough.

CHARLUS

That's what I was thinking.

Another silence.

CHARLUS (*abruptly*)

Good night, sir.

He leaves the room.

130. THE SEA.

MARCEL *swimming.*

Through the froth he sees the little band of GIRLS *walking along the front.*

131. INT. HOTEL. THE LIFT.

>MARCEL *entering the lift.*
>*The lift rises.*
>
>MARCEL *looks through the railings.*
>*On each floor shadowy galleries open out.*
>*A* CHAMBERMAID *comes along one, carrying a bolster.*
>MARCEL *leans forward to look at her.*
>*The lift rises and loses her.*

132. INT. HOTEL. MARCEL'S LANDING.

>MARCEL *leaves the lift.*
>FRANÇOISE *is hurrying along the corridor.*

>>FRANÇOISE

The Marquis de Saint-Loup is going to take a photograph of your grandmother. She's so pleased. She's put on her best dress.

>MARCEL *follows* FRANÇOISE *into* GRANDMOTHER'S *room.*

133. INT. GRANDMOTHER'S ROOM.

>GRANDMOTHER *is sitting at a mirror trying on hats.*

>>GRANDMOTHER

Isn't this silly? The Marquis—

>>MARCEL

I know. I've heard.

>>GRANDMOTHER

Do you mind?

>>MARCEL

It seems a quite frivolous and ridiculous idea to me.

>>FRANÇOISE

O sir, she's going to wear the hat that Françoise has trimmed for her—

MARCEL

Which hat?

FRANÇOISE

The hat she has on.

He does not speak.

GRANDMOTHER

Don't you like it?

MARCEL

Most elegant.

GRANDMOTHER

If you'd rather I didn't—

MARCEL

Please do as you wish. Although I would have thought at your age . . . Well, I'll leave you to adorn yourself.

He goes out.

GRANDMOTHER's face, pained.
She looks at herself in the mirror.

GRANDMOTHER

I look so ill. (*She smiles at* FRANÇOISE.) Thank you, Françoise. The hat will disguise it.

134. EXT. HOTEL.

   SAINT-LOUP *with camera. He takes the photograph.*

135. PHOTOGRAPH OF GRANDMOTHER.

   Her face, in pain, carefully concealed by the shadow of the brim of her hat.

136. INT. DINING ROOM. HOTEL. AFTERNOON.

   The dining room, still, empty.
   The whistle of a steamer far away.

137. CLIFF TOP. BALBEC. LONG SHOT.

   The little band of GIRLS, *sitting on the grass with a picnic.*

138. *THE ROAD TO HUDIMESNIL. DAY.*

> *The* MARQUISE DE VILLEPARISIS's *carriage, containing the* MARQUISE, MARCEL, *and* GRANDMOTHER, *traveling downhill.*
>
> MARCEL *sitting, staring rather vacantly ahead. Suddenly he concentrates, his eyes narrowing.*

139. *THE TREES.*

> *Three trees stand alone at the entrance to an avenue.*

140. *MARCEL'S FACE.*

141. *HIGH SHOT. CARRIAGE ON THE ROAD.*

142. *HIS P.O.V.*

> *The trees, although the carriage is moving away from them, give the impression of following it.*

143. *MARCEL'S FACE, ALIVE.*

144. *THE TREES.*

> *They follow the carriage.*

145. *THE CARRIAGE.*

> MME. DE VILLEPARISIS *and* GRANDMOTHER *regarding gently the passing countryside.*

146. *MARCEL'S FACE, INTENSE.*

147. *FLASH OF THE STEEPLES AT MARTINVILLE.*

148. *THE TREES, WITHDRAWING.*

149. *THE TREES ARE NO LONGER IN SIGHT.*

150. *MARCEL'S FACE.*

>   *He is still looking back.*

151. *THE CARRIAGE.*

>>>   GRANDMOTHER
>   What are you looking at, Marcel?

>>>   MARCEL *(turning)*
>   Nothing.

>>>   MME. DE VILLEPARISIS
>   Have I missed something?

>>>   MARCEL
>   No.

152. *CLOSE SHOT. FLOWERS ON CLIFF TOP.*

>   *Boats on the horizon.*

>   *A butterfly flutters between the flowers.*

>>>   GISÈLE *(V.O.)*
>   Aren't you eating any sandwiches?

153. *EXT. THE CLIFF TOP. BALBEC. DAY.*

>   *The little band of* GIRLS: ALBERTINE *(18),* ANDRÉE
>   *(20),* GISÈLE, ROSEMONDE, *and* DELPHINE *(all 17),*
>   *with* MARCEL, *sitting with a picnic. Hampers, etc. At*
>   *the edge of the field, bicycles.*

>>>   MARCEL
>   No. I prefer this.

>>>   ALBERTINE
>   What is it exactly?

>>>   MARCEL
>   A chocolate cake.

>   *Silence. They all munch.*

>>>   ALBERTINE
>   Don't you actually *like* sandwiches?

50

MARCEL

Not very much.

Silence.

GISÈLE

What do you think of that, Andrée?

ANDRÉE *smiles.*

154. *EXT. EDGE OF A WOOD, NEAR BALBEC. DAY.*

ALBERTINE *sitting with* MARCEL.

ALBERTINE

What did you normally do, before you met us? Just mooch about on the beach all day, with all those old trouts? I mean, don't you like games? We play golf all the time. Of course, most of the other people who play golf are perfectly tedious, perfectly boring.

Pause.

ALBERTINE

I could see you wanted to know us. I could see you were interested in us. But actually, apart from Andrée . . . apart from Andrée, the others are extremely stupid. I suppose you've realized that. They're just children.

155. *ALBERTINE IN PROFILE. HER CHEEKS.*

ALBERTINE

But Andrée is really intelligent. Oh yes. Oh, she's quite intelligent.

156. *ANDRÉE APPROACHES THEM FROM THE WOOD.*

ALBERTINE *jumps up.*

ALBERTINE

Goodness, what's the time? We're supposed to be at tea with Madame Durieux!

ANDRÉE

There's plenty of time.

ALBERTINE

I'm going.

ANDRÉE

I'm staying. To talk to him.

ALBERTINE

You'll be late.

ANDRÉE

Don't be an idiot.

ALBERTINE

Oh, as you like. (*To* MARCEL.) I have a note for you.

She takes an envelope from her bag and hands it to him.

ALBERTINE

Good-bye.

ALBERTINE *goes to her bicycle and rides off.*

157. MARCEL AND ANDRÉE.

MARCEL

Do you mind if I open this?

ANDRÉE

Why not?

He tears open the envelope.

158. CLOSE SHOT. THE LETTER.

It reads: "I like you."

159. MARCEL AND ANDRÉE.

He puts the letter back in the envelope, and into his pocket. He looks up. ANDRÉE *smiles at him.*

ANDRÉE

She's an orphan, you know.

160. EXT. THE PROMENADE. BALBEC. DAY.

>A line of very old ladies sitting in deck chairs on the
>promenade.
>
>Camera finds MARCEL and ALBERTINE standing
>together.

ALBERTINE

I'm staying at your hotel tomorrow night. I'm going
back to Paris. I'm staying at the hotel, so that I can
catch the first train in the morning. You can come and
see me in my room, if you like.

MARCEL

Yes. I'd like to.

ALBERTINE

I'm wearing my hair in the way you like. You did say you
liked it like this, didn't you?

161. EXT. CLIFF TOP. DAY.

>ANDRÉE smiling at him.

162. INT. ALBERTINE'S ROOM. HOTEL. NIGHT.

>MARCEL closing the door, behind him.
>
>ALBERTINE is lying in bed. Her white nightgown
>leaves her throat bare. Her hair is undone.
>
>Beyond the bed, through the window, moon on the
>sea.

ALBERTINE

I went to bed. I had a slight chill.

>MARCEL stares at her.

MARCEL

You're chilly?

ALBERTINE

No, I'm not chilly. I'm quite warm, thank you. I said I

53

felt I had a slight chill, so I got into bed. (*She waves to a chair.*) Sit down.

He sits slowly on the bed.

163. ALBERTINE LYING IN BED.

    She looks up at him.

    He leans towards her, to kiss her.

ALBERTINE

Stop that, or I'll ring the bell!

164. HIS FACE.

    He pauses, regards her for a moment, and then leans towards her again, decisively. As his lips touch her turning face he hears the shrill sound of the bell.

165. ALBERTINE'S ARM TUGGING THE BELL.

166. HEDGE AT TANSONVILLE.

    GILBERTE *looking at him through the hedge.*

167. WINDOW AT MONTJOUVAIN.

    MLLE. VINTEUIL *running to window to close the shutters. Her* FRIEND *on sofa in background.*

168. FLASH OF YELLOW SCREEN.

    Music of Vinteuil.

169. INT. DRAWING ROOM. NEW FLAT IN PARIS IN A WING OF THE DUC DE GUERMANTES'S HOUSE. DAY. LATE 1898.

    GRANDMOTHER *is sitting under a lamp, a book on her lap. She is reading, but halfheartedly, her eyes continually lifting from the page, her head slightly nodding.*

She looks heavy, old, ill.

Suddenly she turns towards the camera, smiles with an effort.

170. INT. DRAWING ROOM. NEW FLAT. DAY. LATE 1898. A FEW WEEKS EARLIER THAN PREVIOUS SHOT.

> *The room is in a certain amount of disarray, showing evidence of a recent move.*
>
> MARCEL *is standing at the window, looking down on the courtyard. He is nineteen.*
>
> FRANÇOISE *and a* FOOTMAN *are fixing a painting to the wall.*

171. OVER MARCEL TO COURTYARD.

> JUPIEN (49) *is passing. He looks up, smiles, lifts his hat, goes towards his shop.*

FRANÇOISE (V.O.)
He's the only friendly man I've met around here so far. The only person of any charm.

MARCEL
Who is it?

FRANÇOISE (V.O.)
Monsieur Jupien. He's a tailor. That's his shop.

172. EXT. COURTYARD. MARCEL'S P.O.V.

> JUPIEN *enters his shop.*
>
> *Horses are being led by grooms to stables.*

173. INT. DRAWING ROOM.

> MOTHER *joins* MARCEL *at the window.*

MOTHER
Isn't it strange? You remember when you were a little

boy, the magic the name Guermantes had for you? And now here you are living so close to them.

Pause.

MARCEL

Very strange.

174. INT. COMBRAY CHURCH. 1893.

> The DUCHESSE *(35), turning, smiling.*

175. INT. BOX AT THE OPERA. 1898.

> The DUCHESSE *lifting her gloved hand, waving.*
> The PRINCESSE *turns to look down.*

176. INT. THE GUERMANTES' HOUSE. THE HALL. DAY.

> The DUCHESSE *in the hall, at a mirror, adjusting her hat, smoothing her cuffs. Her hair is golden.*
> *She leaves the house. The servants bow.*

177. EXT. COURTYARD GATE. THE GUERMANTES' HOUSE.

> The PORTER *opens the gates, bowing, as the DUCHESSE passes.*
> Camera *stays with the* DUCHESSE *as she walks down the street. Her eyes suddenly see someone.*
> *She nods curtly, walks on.*
> Camera *pans to find* MARCEL, *standing, looking after her.*

178. EXT. A BOULEVARD.

> The DUCHESSE *walking.*
> *She looks sharply to her right.*

179. *HER EYES.*

180. *MARCEL. STANDING BY A TREE.*

    He bows, lifts his hat.

181. *THE DUCHESSE, WALKING.*

    She nods, curtly. Her face is sullen.

182. *EXT. PASTRY COOK'S SHOP.*

    Through the window the Duchesse *seen pointing to cakes. The assistant begins to wrap them. The Du-chesse's eyes stray to the window. She stares, turns away, abruptly.*

183. *INT. THEATER. THE STAGE: BACKSTAGE STOR-AGE AREA. LATE 1898.*

    The curtain is down. Stagehands are moving scenery. It is the interval.

    Saint-Loup *and* Marcel *walk onto the stage.*

Saint-Loup

What did you think?

Marcel

She has a wonderful stage presence.

Saint-Loup

She has. It's electric. She's beautiful too, isn't she?

Marcel

Very striking.

    Stagehands continue their work.

    Three Journalists *appear on the stage, one smok-ing a cigar.*

Saint-Loup (to Marcel)

She'll be here in a minute. She's dying to meet you.

    Pause.

MARCEL

While we're waiting, I wanted to ask you something.

SAINT-LOUP

Yes?

MARCEL

Your aunt, the Duchesse de Guermantes . . .

SAINT-LOUP

Yes?

MARCEL

I believe she thinks I'm an idiot.

SAINT-LOUP

What makes you say that?

MARCEL

A rumor . . . that's all.

SAINT-LOUP

Rubbish. Have you met her?

MARCEL

No.

SAINT-LOUP

I'll introduce you.

MARCEL

When?

SAINT-LOUP

When I get the chance.

SAINT-LOUP *walks up and down the stage.*

SAINT-LOUP

Where is she?

One or two actors and dancers appear in the wings. A man approaches the JOURNALISTS *in background and questions them. One of the* JOURNALISTS *is heard to say:*

JOURNALIST

We're waiting for Monsieur Bouvet.

SAINT-LOUP (*to* MARCEL, *vaguely*)

How's the writing?

MARCEL

I'm not doing any.

RACHEL *appears.*

SAINT-LOUP

Darling. (*He kisses her.*) You were wonderful. This is
Marcel. Marcel—Rachel.

They shake hands.

MARCEL

Congratulations.

RACHEL

Did you enjoy it?

MARCEL

Very much.

SAINT-LOUP

You were wonderful.

RACHEL

Oh don't be ridiculous. How could I be wonderful in
such a small part? Next season I'll be playing leads.
Then you can judge.

During this speech RACHEL's *gaze has been straying
to a male* DANCER, *practicing on the side of the
stage.*

SAINT-LOUP

What are you looking at?

RACHEL

Mmmnn?

SAINT-LOUP

Why are you looking at him?

RACHEL

Who?

SAINT-LOUP

That damn dancer.

RACHEL

Was I?

Stagehands, in moving scenery, press SAINT-LOUP, RACHEL, *and* MARCEL *closer to the group of* JOURNAL-ISTS, *who listen with interest to the conversation.*

RACHEL

Why shouldn't I? Look how beautifully made he is. And look at his hands.

The DANCER *is dressed as a Watteau page, his eyelids stiff with paint, his cheeks plastered with rouge. Hearing* RACHEL's *remarks, he very delicately repeats the movements of his hands.*

RACHEL

How exquisite.

SAINT-LOUP

If you don't stop this I'll leave at once, do you understand? (*To* MARCEL.) You shouldn't stand about in the cigar smoke like this. It'll make you ill.

RACHEL (*to* SAINT-LOUP)

Oh, go then, for goodness' sake!

SAINT-LOUP

If I go I won't come back.

RACHEL

Good.

SAINT-LOUP (*whispering*)

I promised you that necklace, if you remember—

RACHEL

Don't try to blackmail me! I'm not a moneygrubber. Keep your necklace.

SAINT-LOUP

You want me to leave you then? Is that what you want?

RACHEL

Isn't he wonderful with his hands?

MARCEL *coughs.*

SAINT-LOUP (*to* JOURNALIST)

Would you mind putting out your cigar, sir? The smoke is bad for my friend.

RACHEL (*to* DANCER)

Do they do those tricks with women too, those lovely hands? They're girl's hands. I'm sure I could have a wonderful time with you and a girl I know.

184. *C.U. THE DANCER.*

He is smiling.

185. *THE STAGE.*

RACHEL *walks slowly into the wings.*

JOURNALIST

There's no rule against smoking, as far as I know. He's not forced to stay here, is he?

SAINT-LOUP (*politely*)

I'm afraid you are not very civil, sir.

SAINT-LOUP *raises his arm and hits the* JOURNALIST *with extreme force across the face. The* JOURNALIST *staggers back. His* COLLEAGUES *turn away. One rubs his eye, as if dust had entered it. The other looks at his watch.*

SECOND JOURNALIST

Good gracious, the curtain's going up in a minute. We shan't get to our seats.

SAINT-LOUP *strides out.* MARCEL *follows him.*

186. *QUICK SHOT.*

The DANCER, *moving his hands.*

187. *EXT. STAGE DOOR OF THEATER. EVENING.*

>MARCEL *comes out of stage door.*
>He sees SAINT-LOUP *walking up the street.*
>A MAN *approaches* SAINT-LOUP, *who stops. The*
>MAN *begins to speak rapidly to him.*
>
>SAINT-LOUP *suddenly hits him a number of times,*
>*knocking him down. He turns, sees* MARCEL, *joins*
>*him. They walk in the opposite direction.*

>SAINT-LOUP

Damn filth! He made a proposition to me! Can you
imagine it? In broad daylight! They don't even wait for
night to fall now, the scum!

188. *INT. THE FLAT. DAY. (SAME AS SHOT NO. 169.)*

>GRANDMOTHER *sitting under lamp with book.*
>*She turns to the camera, smiles.*

>GRANDMOTHER

Hullo, Marcel.

189. *EXT. STREET. DAY. 1899.*

>MARCEL *(19) walking towards the house of* MME. DE
>VILLEPARISIS.

190. *INT. MME. DE VILLEPARISIS'S DRAWING ROOM.*
DAY. 1899.

>*The drawing room is hung with yellow silk, sofas*
>*upholstered in Beauvais tapestry. Many portraits.*
>
>MME. DE VILLEPARISIS *is seated at a desk dressed in a*
>*cap of black lace, spectacles, and an apron.*
>
>*On the desk are paintbrushes, a palette, and an*
>*unfinished watercolor, and in glasses, saucers, and*
>*cups are moss roses, zinnias, and maidenhair ferns.*
>
>*She is painting. Some people stand around the desk,*

watching, including MARCEL; *various others are about the room, talking.*

A BUTLER *is serving tea and cakes.*

MME. DE VILLEPARISIS

Yes, I remember Monsieur Molé very well. He was extraordinarily pompous. I can see him now coming downstairs to dinner in his own house with his hat in his hand.

AN HISTORIAN

Was that a common habit at the time, madame?

MME. DE VILLEPARISIS

Not at all. It was just a habit Monsieur Molé had, that's all. I never saw my father carry his hat in the house, except of course when the King came, because the King being at home wherever he is, the master of the house is a visitor in his own drawing room.

The FOOTMAN *at the door announces: "The Duchesse de Guermantes."*

The DUCHESSE *(41) walks across the room to* MME. DE VILLEPARISIS.

MME. DE VILLEPARISIS

How are you, Oriane? (*To the small group.*) Let me introduce my niece, the Duchesse de Guermantes.

The DUCHESSE *bows very quickly and coldly to them.*

FOOTMAN *at the door announces: "The Comte d'Argencourt."*

191. *THE DUCHESSE DE GUERMANTES.*

She sits alone on a sofa. She wears a straw hat trimmed with cornflowers and a blue striped silk skirt.
With the point of her sunshade she traces circles on the carpet.

Her eyes then inspect each sofa and swiftly its occupant.

192. MARCEL.

He stands alone, watching her.

193. AT THE DOOR OF THE ROOM.

Two Young Men are at the door. They are both tall, slender, golden-haired. The Footman, who is also young, announces: "The Prince de Foix." The Prince passes into the room.

The Footman and the other Young Man suddenly stare at each other in recognition. The Footman's eyes are wide. The Young Man quickly closes his.

FOOTMAN (*in a low voice*)
Your name, sir?

YOUNG MAN (*in a lower voice*)
The Duc de Châtellerault.

The Footman turns to the room and announces with pride: "His Royal Highness, the Duc de Châtellerault."

194. THE DUCHESSE ON THE SOFA.

The Prince and the Duc kiss her hand and sit on either side of her, laying their silk hats on the floor by their feet.

The Historian looks at the hats.

HISTORIAN
I don't think you should leave your hats on the floor, gentlemen. They might be trodden on.

195. *C.U. THE PRINCE DE FOIX.*

> *He stares at the* Historian, *his eyes piercing, very cold.*

196. *THE HISTORIAN.*

> *He flushes, stammers, turns away.*

197. *THE SOFA.*

>> Prince de Foix (*to the* Duchesse)
>
> Who is that person? The person who just addressed me.
>
>> Duchesse
>
> I haven't the slightest idea.
>
> *She turns to* Châtellerault, *who is sitting with his eyes closed.*
>
>> Duchesse
>
> You look dreadfully pale, Châtellerault. Are you ill?
>
>> Châtellerault (*without opening his eyes*)
>
> Hay fever.

198. *MME. DE VILLEPARISIS, PAINTING.*

> *The* Butler *brings to her a card on a tray. She looks at it.*
>
>> Mme. de Villeparisis
>
> The Queen of Sweden! Good gracious. I had no idea she knew I was back in Paris.
>
> Footman *at door announces: "Her Majesty, the Queen of Sweden."*
>
> *Enter the* Duc de Guermantes. *He roars with laughter.*
>
> *General laughter.*
>
> *The* Duc *approaches* Mme. de Villeparisis, *greeting people as he walks, shaking hands.*
> *He kisses* Mme. de Villeparisis*'s hand.*

Duc

I thought you'd be amused.

Mme. de Villeparisis (*unamused*)

What an idiotic joke.

The Duc *laughs.*

Duc

I knew it would amuse you.

He sees Marcel.

Duc

Ah, my neighbor! How do you do?

Marcel *bows.*

Duchesse

We met the Queen last night as a matter of fact at Blanche Lord's. She's grown absolutely enormous.

Duc

Oriane said she looked like a frog.

Duchesse

A frog in an "interesting condition."

Laughter.

199. *MARCEL, UNSMILING.*

200. *THE ROOM.*

Footman *announces: "The Baron de Charlus."*

The camera glimpses Charlus *through the now packed gathering.*

Marcel *turns to find* M. de Norpois *beside him.*

Norpois

Writing anything these days?

Norpois *is greeted by someone else and turns away.*

Mme. de Villeparisis *leans towards the* Duchesse.

66

MME. DE VILLEPARISIS
I think you should know that I am expecting Madame Swann to visit me this afternoon.

DUCHESSE
Oh really? Thank you for telling me.

The DUCHESSE *turns abruptly to look for the first time at* MARCEL.

DUCHESSE
Good afternoon. How are you?

MARCEL
Thank you, madame. I am quite well.

FOOTMAN's *voice announcing: "The Prince von Faffenheim-Munsterburg-Weinigen."*

The DUCHESSE *regards* MARCEL.

DUCHESSE
I see you sometimes in the morning. It's so good for one, a walk.

FOOTMAN *announces: "Madame Charles Swann."*

The DUCHESSE *looks at her watch.*

DUCHESSE
Gracious, I must fly.

She stands, and moves swiftly away.

MARCEL *wanders through the now very crowded room, carefully stepping over the long skirts of the ladies and avoiding the crowd of hats that litter the carpet.*

Around him an intense chatter of conversation; indecipherable.

He glimpses CHARLUS *talking to* ODETTE *on a sofa.*

He turns to see the DUC DE CHÂTELLERAULT *and the* PRINCE DE FOIX *sitting erect and silent.*

67

201. *INT. MARCEL'S BEDROOM. COMBRAY. 1888.*
    (SAME AS SHOT NO. 53.)

> The magic lantern.
> The image of Geneviève de Brabant floats over the
> walls and ceiling.

202. *INT. MME. DE VILLEPARISIS'S DRAWING ROOM.*

> MARCEL *draws near to* MME. DE VILLEPARISIS, *still
> painting, watched by a circle of admirers.*
>
> He is tapped on the shoulder. He turns. It is
> CHARLUS.

CHARLUS

As I see you've taken to going into society you must do
me the pleasure of coming to see me. But it's a little
complicated. I am seldom at home. You will have to
write to me. I am just going. Will you walk a short way
with me?

MARCEL

Certainly.

CHARLUS

Wait for me.

> CHARLUS *turns away.*
>
> MME. DE VILLEPARISIS *has overheard these remarks.
> She beckons* MARCEL *to her, speaks quietly.*

MME. DE VILLEPARISIS

You are leaving with my nephew?

MARCEL

Yes, he has asked me to walk home with him.

MME. DE VILLEPARISIS

Don't wait for him. He's busy talking. He's certain to
have forgotten what he said to you. Go now quickly
while his back is turned.

203. *INT. MME. DE VILLEPARISIS'S HOUSE. THE STAIRCASE.*

> MARCEL *descending the staircase alone.*
>
> CHARLUS's *voice from the top of the stairs.*
>
> #### CHARLUS'S VOICE
> So this is how you wait for me, is it?
>
> MARCEL *turns to see* CHARLUS *staring down at him.*

204. *EXT. STREET.*

> MARCEL *and* CHARLUS *come out of the house.*
>
> #### CHARLUS
> We'll walk a little way, until I find a cab that suits me.
>
> *They walk.*
>
> #### CHARLUS
> What in heaven's name were you doing at that idiotic tea party? It's a complete waste of your time. I know I was there myself, but for me it was not a social gathering—simply a family visit.
>
> CHARLUS *stares at a passing cab. The driver stops.*
> CHARLUS *waves him on. They continue walking.*
>
> #### CHARLUS
> What nonsense the newspapers talk about that fellow Dreyfus. How can one charge Dreyfus with betraying his country? He's a Jew, not a Frenchman. The only sensible charge against him would be one of infringing the laws of hospitality.
>
> CHARLUS *pauses in his step to stare at another passing cab. The driver stops.* CHARLUS *waves him on.* MARCEL *looks at him, questioningly.*
>
> #### CHARLUS
> I didn't like the color of his lamps.
>
> *They walk.*

CHARLUS

I will ask you a simple question. Are you worth my trouble or not?

MARCEL

I am very grateful . . . that you should take an interest in me.

CHARLUS *clasps his arm.*

CHARLUS

Your words touch me.

They walk arm in arm.

CHARLUS

I think I can help you. I do not, as a rule, care to talk about myself, but you may possibly have heard—it was referred to in a leading article in *The Times*, which made a considerable impression—that the Emperor of Austria, who has always honored me with his friendship, said the other day in an interview that if the Comte de Chambord had been advised by a man as thoroughly conversant with the undercurrents of European politics as myself he would be King of France today.

CHARLUS *looks at* MARCEL. MARCEL *looks at* CHARLUS.

CHARLUS

The fact is, I have within me an invaluable secret record which it has taken me over thirty years to collect. I could hand it over to a deserving young man in a few months. I have but one passion left, to seek to redeem the mistakes of my life by conferring the benefit of my knowledge on a soul that is still virgin. But if you are to be that young man, I would have to see you often, very often, every day.

CHARLUS *stops walking, and looks into* MARCEL'S *eyes, still clasping his arm.*

He abruptly drops MARCEL'S *arm and continues walking.* MARCEL *follows.*

A cab passes.
In it MARCEL *sees the* COMTE D'ARGENCOURT, *looking at them.*
CHARLUS *continues speaking as if there had been no pause.*

CHARLUS

For the time being, you must keep out of society. Parties like the one we've just left will warp your intellect and character. And be very careful in choosing your friends. Keep mistresses if you like, that doesn't concern me (*he squeezes his arm*), you young rascal, but your choice of men friends is more important. My nephew Saint-Loup is a suitable companion for you. At least he's a man, not one of those effeminate creatures who abound today, little whores who so casually bring their innocent victims to the gallows.

A cab approaches, zigzagging along the street.
The young CABMAN *is driving it from inside the cab, sprawling across the cushions.*

CHARLUS *stops the cab.*

CABMAN (*drunkenly*)

Which way are you going?

CHARLUS

Yours.

CABMAN

I'm driving it from down here. It's up to you.

CHARLUS

Put the hood up.

The CABMAN *staggers to put up the hood.*

CHARLUS (*to* MARCEL)

I give you a few days to think about my offer. Consider it most seriously.

He bows quickly and goes to the cab.

He helps the CABMAN *to put up the hood, climbs in with him, and takes the reins.*

CHARLUS

I'll drive.

The horse trots off.

205. *INT. MARCEL'S FLAT. GRANDMOTHER'S ROOM. DAY. 1899.*

MOTHER *is helping* GRANDMOTHER *into her cloak.*

MOTHER

A walk will do you good.

GRANDMOTHER

Yes.

MOTHER

The doctor said it would be good for you. It's a lovely day.

GRANDMOTHER

Yes. Yes, it is.

The door opens. MARCEL *comes in.*

MARCEL

Oh, come on. I've been waiting for you for hours.

GRANDMOTHER

Yes, yes. I'm coming. It is a lovely day.

MARCEL

It'll probably be pouring with rain by the time we get there.

MOTHER

No, no, it won't. (*To* GRANDMOTHER.) It'll be good for you. The air will do you good.

206. *EXT. AVENUE GABRIEL. DAY.*

A cab stops. MARCEL *and* GRANDMOTHER *get out. They walk slowly along the treelined path.*

MARCEL

Not a bad day, is it?

> GRANDMOTHER, *without speaking, suddenly turns away and heads for a public lavatory; a pavilion covered with green trellis.*

> *The female attendant, known as* LA MARQUISE, *is sitting outside talking to a park keeper. She stands, takes* GRANDMOTHER *inside.*

> MARCEL *climbs the steps and stands, waiting.*
> LA MARQUISE *returns and sits again.*

LA MARQUISE

What was I saying?

PARK KEEPER

About the magistrate.

LA MARQUISE

That's right. For the last eight years that man has been here every day at the stroke of three. Always a perfect gentleman. Stays half an hour, reads his papers, goes away satisfied. It's like a haven for him, my little place, my little piece of Paris. One day he didn't come. I thought he must have died. But the next day there he was again, right on the stroke of three. "I hope nothing happened to you yesterday," I said. But he told me nothing had happened to him, it was just that his wife had died. I said to him: "You just keep coming here, the same as before, and it'll be a little distraction for you in your sorrow."

> *Pause.*

LA MARQUISE

I choose my customers. I don't let everyone come into my little parlors.

> *She turns to* MARCEL.

LA MARQUISE

You wouldn't like me to open a little place for you?

> MARCEL

No, thank you.

> LA MARQUISE

You're quite welcome, as my guest. But, of course, not having to pay for a thing won't make you want to do anything if you've got nothing to do.

> GRANDMOTHER *comes out, slowly. She gives* LA MARQUISE *some money.*

> LA MARQUISE

Thank you, madame. Have a nice walk.

207. *EXT. THE AVENUE.*

> MARCEL *and* GRANDMOTHER *walking, slowly.*

> GRANDMOTHER

I heard what she was saying. Could anything be more like the Guermantes, the Verdurins? Exactly the same.

> GRANDMOTHER *has spoken with great difficulty, wincing, clenching her teeth. Her hat is crooked, her cloak stained. She looks dazed.*

> MARCEL *looks at her closely. He speaks cheerfully.*

> MARCEL

It's getting cold. I suggest we go home.

> GRANDMOTHER

Yes.

> MARCEL

We'll just find a cab and be home in next to no time.

> GRANDMOTHER

Yes.

> *She smiles and grips his hand.*
> *He leads her to a bench.*

> MARCEL

You sit down here. I'll find the cab.

GRANDMOTHER

Yes.

She sits, but does not let go of his hand, looking up at him. He gently loosens her grip.

MARCEL

I'll look for the cab.

GRANDMOTHER

Yes.

208. INT. FLAT. MARCEL'S ROOM. NIGHT.

He is in bed.
The door opens. MOTHER *enters. She goes to the bed, looks down at him, her face drained.*

MOTHER

I'm sorry . . . to disturb your sleep.

He looks up at her.

MARCEL

I wasn't asleep.

He gets out of bed.

209. INT. GRANDMOTHER'S BEDROOM. NIGHT.

DR. COTTARD, MARCEL'S FATHER, FRANÇOISE, *are in the room.*
MARCEL *and* MOTHER *enter.*

GRANDMOTHER, *in the bed, is having convulsions.*
The oxygen cylinder is at work.
The blankets heave. Her hands keep trying to thrust them aside, impotently. Her hair is wild.

She suddenly groans violently and lurches into a sitting position. Both eyes are closed, but one eyelid is not completely down.

She lurches forward again.

The chink of her left eye, filmy, dim. She groans.

Abruptly she is still.

Both her eyes open, very clear.

210. INT. MARCEL'S ROOM. HIS WRITING DESK. 1900.

> *Hands opening two envelopes.*
>
> *The first is an invitation to* Marcel *to dinner from the* Duchesse de Guermantes.
>
> *The second is a note from* Charlus *asking* Marcel *to visit him the same night, at eleven o'clock.*

211. EXT. COURTYARD. NIGHT.

> Marcel *walking across the courtyard towards the brightly lit Guermantes' house.*
>
> *Carriages arriving through the gates.*

212. INT. THE GUERMANTES' DRAWING ROOM. 1900. (SILENT.)

> Marcel *is being introduced by the* Duc *to a group of ladies. They all have bare bosoms, to which are attached sprays of mimosa, roses, garlands of orchids. They appear to respond to* Marcel *seductively, coyly, mischievously.*

213. INT. THE GUERMANTES' DINING ROOM. (SILENT.)

> *Dinner being served.*
>
> *Various shots of the diners.*
>
> *The* Duc *looking with a slight smile at a young lady who is aware of his look.*
>
> *The* Duchesse *says something dryly. Everyone laughs.*
>
> *The* Duc *glances with irritation at the* Duchesse, *gestures to a waiter for more meat.*
>
> Marcel, *bosoms heaving on either side of him.*

214. EXT. THE GUERMANTES' GARDEN. NIGHT. (SILENT.)

> *The guests sipping orange juice and liqueurs, sitting, walking.*
>
> *Musicians play.*
>
> *The DUC talking to the young lady.*
>
> *MARCEL alone on a bench. The DUCHESSE comes to sit next to him. She wears a very wide dress. He stands for her to sit, sits again on the end of the bench and nearly falls off.*

215. INT. BARON DE CHARLUS'S HOUSE. THE BARON'S ROOM. NIGHT.

> *CHARLUS, in a Chinese dressing gown, throat bare, is lying on a sofa.*
>
> *The VALET shows MARCEL into the room and withdraws.*
>
> *A tall hat, its top flashing in the light, sits on a cape on a chair.*
>
> *CHARLUS stares at MARCEL in silence.*

MARCEL

Good evening.

> *No reply. The stare is implacable.*

MARCEL

May I sit down?

> *Silence.*

CHARLUS

Take the Louis Quatorze chair.

> *MARCEL sits abruptly in a Directoire chair beside him.*

CHARLUS

Ah! So that is what you call a Louis Quatorze chair! I can see you have been well educated. One of these days you'll take Madame de Villeparisis's lap for a lavatory and goodness knows what you'll do in it.

Pause.

CHARLUS

Sir, this interview which I have condescended to grant you will mark the end of our relationship.

He stretches an arm along the back of the sofa.

CHARLUS

Since I was everything and you were nothing, since I, if I may state it plainly, am a prodigious personage and you in comparison a microbe, it was naturally I who took the first steps towards you. You have made an imbecilic reply to what it is not for me to describe as an act of greatness. In short, you have lied about me to others. You have repeated calumnies against me to others. Therefore these are the last words we shall exchange on this earth.

Pause.

MARCEL

Never, sir. I have never spoken about you to anyone.

CHARLUS

You left unanswered the proposal I made to you here in Paris. The idea did not attract you. There is no more to be said about that. But that you did not take the trouble to write to me shows that you lack not only breeding, good manners, sensibility, but common or garden intelligence. Instead, you prove yourself despicable in speaking of me disrespectfully to the world at large.

MARCEL

Sir, I swear to you that I have said nothing to anyone that could insult you.

CHARLUS (*with extreme violence*)

Insult me? Who says that I am insulted? Do you suppose it is within your power to insult me? You

78

evidently do not realize to whom you are speaking. Do you imagine that the envenomed spittle of five hundred little gentlemen of your type, heaped one upon the other, would succeed in slobbering so much as the tips of my august toes?

MARCEL *stares at him, jumps up, seizes the* BARON'*s silk hat, throws it down, tramples it, picks it up, wrenches off the brim, tears the crown in two.*

CHARLUS

What in heaven's name are you doing? Have you gone mad?

MARCEL *rushes to the door and opens it.*

TWO FOOTMEN *are standing outside. They move slowly away.*

MARCEL *walks quickly past them, followed by* CHARLUS, *who bars his way.*

CHARLUS

There, there, don't be childish. Come back for a minute. He that loveth well chasteneth well. I have chastened you well because I love you well.

He draws MARCEL *back into the room.*

CHARLUS (*to* FOOTMAN)

Take away the hat and bring me a new one.

CHARLUS *and* MARCEL *stand as the* FOOTMAN *collects the pieces of the hat together.*

MARCEL

I would like to know the name of your informer, sir.

CHARLUS

I have given a promise of secrecy to my *informant.* I do not intend to betray that promise.

MARCEL

You insult me, sir. I have already sworn to you that I have said nothing.

CHARLUS (*thunderously*)

Are you calling me a liar?

MARCEL

You have been misinformed.

CHARLUS

It is quite possible. Generally speaking, a remark repeated at second hand is rarely true. But true or false,
the remark has done its work.

Pause.

MARCEL

I had better go.

CHARLUS

I agree. Or, if you feel too tired, I have plenty of beds
here.

MARCEL

Thank you. I am not too tired.

CHARLUS

It is true that my affection for you is dead. Nothing can
revive it. As Victor Hugo's Boaz said: "I am widowed,
alone, and the dark gathers o'er me."

216. INT. CHARLUS'S HOUSE. DRAWING ROOM.

CHARLUS *and* MARCEL *walking through the green
room.*
*Music is heard from another floor. A Beethoven
romance.*
CHARLUS *points at two portraits.*

CHARLUS

My uncles. The King of Poland and the King of
England.

217. EXT. CHARLUS'S HOUSE. THE FRONT DOOR.

The carriage waits. CHARLUS *and* MARCEL *look up at
the night sky.*

CHARLUS

What a superb moon. I think I shall take a walk in the
Bois.

MARCEL *does not respond to this.*

CHARLUS

It would be pleasant to walk in the Bois under the moon
with someone like yourself. For you're charming, really,
quite charming. When I met you first I must confess I
found you quite insignificant.

He takes MARCEL *to his carriage.* MARCEL *gets in.*

CHARLUS

Remember this. Affection is precious. Do not neglect it.
Thank you for coming. Good night.

218. *CHARLUS AT FRONT DOOR. NIGHT.*

His face. Impassive.

Sound of carriage departing.

219. *EXT. THE GUERMANTES' COURTYARD. DAY.*

CHARLUS, *in a dark suit, looking at something, his
face curiously soft.*

220. *INT. WINDOW OF MARCEL'S FLAT. DAY.*

The shutters are ajar.

Through the shutters CHARLUS *can be seen looking
at* JUPIEN, *who has just come out of his shop.*

JUPIEN, *aware of* CHARLUS's *gaze, returns it.*
CHARLUS *turns his head to look carelessly around the
courtyard, his gaze regularly returning to* JUPIEN. *His
gaze is searching.*

JUPIEN *puts his hand on his hip, sticks out his
buttocks, inclines his head to one side, holds the
pose.*

CHARLUS *casually approaches him. They stand close
to each other for a moment in silence.*

81

CHARLUS
Do you by any chance have a light?

JUPIEN
Of course.

CHARLUS
Unfortunately I've left my cigars at home.

JUPIEN
Come inside. I have cigars.

They go into the shop. The door shuts.

221. EXT. THE EMPTY COURTYARD.

MARCEL *comes out of his door.*
He strolls round the courtyard, keeping close to the walls, apparently deep in thought.
When he reaches the shop next to JUPIEN'S *he casually opens the door and goes in.*

222. INT. VACANT PREMISES OF SHOP.

MARCEL *stands quite still in the gloom by a partition, on the other side of which is* JUPIEN'S *shop.*
Violent inarticulate sexual sounds emerge from behind the partition.
Gasps. A sudden silence.
Sound of running water.
Voices:

JUPIEN
No, I don't want any money. It was my pleasure.

Water.

JUPIEN
Why do you shave your chin like that? A nice beard is so becoming.

82

CHARLUS

A nice beard is disgusting. Listen. You don't know anything about the man who sells chestnuts round the corner, not the one on the left, he's a horror, but the other one, a big dark fellow?

JUPIEN

You're heartless.

A scrape of furniture, a squeal from JUPIEN, *sudden silence.*

JUPIEN (*short of breath*)

You're very naughty. You're a big baby.

MARCEL *climbs a ladder and peers down through a ventilator into the other shop.*

CHARLUS *is moving away from* JUPIEN. *He sits and lights a cigar.*

CHARLUS

Do you know any ticket collectors, by any chance? I often need entertainment on my homeward journeys. You see, it falls to my lot, now and then, like the caliph who used to roam the streets of Bagdad in the guise of a common merchant, to condescend to follow some curious little person whose profile may have taken my fancy. He takes a tram. I follow. He takes a train. I follow. But more often than not I find myself at the end of the line at eleven o'clock at night with nothing to show for it. That's why I should like to get to know a ticket collector or a sleeping car attendant, to console me on my way home.

He looks sharply at JUPIEN.

CHARLUS

You could be my agent! A brilliant idea. You could· render me great service.

JUPIEN

Could I?

CHARLUS

Indisputably. You're a man of sensitivity and perspicacity. It shines out of your face.

JUPIEN

How sweet of you to say so.

223. *INT. MARCEL'S BEDROOM. PARIS. DUSK. 1900.*

MARCEL *(20) is in bed.* ALBERTINE *(20) sits in a chair by the bed.*

ALBERTINE

And are you well?

MARCEL

Fairly well. I get bouts, from time to time.

ALBERTINE

But you have to rest, like this?

MARCEL

Yes.

ALBERTINE

My poor boy.

She looks at watch.

ALBERTINE

I can't stay long.

MARCEL

You've only just come.

ALBERTINE

Yes, but I can't be late.

MARCEL

Where are you going?

ALBERTINE

Oh, I have to see some friends.

Pause.

ALBERTINE

I like your room. It's nice. (*She looks at him.*) I thought
you might have grown a moustache.

MARCEL

I prefer to be clean shaven.

ALBERTINE

Moustaches can be nice.

Pause.

ALBERTINE

Do you ever think about Balbec, the sea?

MARCEL

Sometimes.

Pause.

MARCEL

The last time we saw each other you were in bed and I
was sitting on the bed.

ALBERTINE

That's right.

MARCEL

Well, I think you should come and sit on the bed now
and that will make a proper symmetry.

ALBERTINE

A proper what?

MARCEL (*patting bed*)

Sit here.

ALBERTINE (*slowly doing so*)

Here?

MARCEL

Now I can see you.

ALBERTINE

You could see me as easily before.

MARCEL

I can see your eyes better now.

> *Pause.*

MARCEL

You'd be more comfortable, though, if you lay down.

ALBERTINE

Do you think so?

MARCEL

Try it.

ALBERTINE

I have to go soon, you know.

> *She lies down by him, on her front, half over him.*
>
> *Sound of the door opening.*
>
> ALBERTINE *jumps off the bed, falls into her chair.*
>
> FRANÇOISE *comes in, carrying a lamp. She stops.*

MARCEL

The lamp already! Early, isn't it?

FRANÇOISE

Do you want me to put it out?

> ALBERTINE *giggles.*

MARCEL

No. Leave it.

> FRANÇOISE *puts lamp down and leaves.*
>
> ALBERTINE *slowly stands, sits on bed, lies by his side.*

MARCEL

I don't think I can resist the temptation to kiss you.

ALBERTINE

It would be a pity if you did.

> *He draws her towards him.*

224.   *EXT. BEACH. BALBEC. DAY. 1898.*

> ALBERTINE *outlined against the sea and sky, laughing.*

225. *INT. MARCEL'S BEDROOM. DUSK. 1900.*

> Marcel *drawing* Albertine *towards him.*
>
> *Her cheeks, smooth and flushed, come closer to his eye and show a coarser grain.*
>
> *Their lips meet. Darkness.*
> *After a long kiss he whispers:*

Marcel

Why didn't you let me kiss you at Balbec?

Albertine (whispering)

I didn't know you properly.

226. *MARCEL AND ALBERTINE KISSING.*

> *She leans over him, crushing him.*
> *The camera concentrates on their heads only.*
>
> *Suddenly he clutches her. They are still.*

227. *ANOTHER VIEW OF THE BED.*

> *They lie together.*
>
> Albertine's *face is docile, relaxed, abstracted.*

Marcel

Do you have to go?

Albertine

No, no. I have plenty of time.

> *She regards him.*

Albertine

What lovely hair you have, and eyes. You're a sweet boy.

228. *INT. DUC DE GUERMANTES'S HOUSE. FIRST LANDING. DAY. 1900.*

> *The* Duc de Guermantes *is standing at the door of the library.*

DUC

Marcel! How nice of you to look in.

They shake hands.

DUC

Oriane will be here in a moment.

They walk into the library.

229. *INT. LIBRARY. DAY.*

DUC

She's changing. We're dining with Madame de Saint-Euverte, and then we're going to a rather grand party at my cousin's—the Prince de Guermantes. And then we have to be back here by midnight to change again for a very important fancy dress ball given by the Marquise d'Arpajon. I'm going as Louis XI, and Oriane is Isabel of Bavaria. Charles, have you met this young man?

MARCEL *turns to see* SWANN *at the far end of the library.*
SWANN *comes towards him. He is fifty-two. His face is haggard.*
SWANN *looks doubtfully at* MARCEL. *They shake hands.*

SWANN

How do you do?

MARCEL

I'm amazed that you remember me, sir.

SWANN

Of course I do. Of course I do. Are your people well?

MARCEL

They are, thank you.

SWANN

Good, good.

SWANN *wears a pearl gray frockcoat, white gloves*

stitched in black and carries a gray very wide hat,
lined with green leather.

DUC

Charles, you're an expert. I want your opinion of this.

He leads them to a painting.

DUC

What do you think of it? I've just swapped it for a
couple of Monets. I think it might be a Vermeer. What
do you think?

SWANN

Difficult to say.

DUC

Oh come on, we all know you're an expert. You're
writing a book about Vermeer, aren't you?

SWANN

Oh, hardly a book ... Just an article, about one
painting.

MARCEL

View of Delft?

SWANN

Yes.

MARCEL

That patch of yellow wall.

SWANN

Yes.

DUC

Patch? What patch?

SWANN *suddenly recognizes* MARCEL.

MARCEL *turns to the* DUC.

MARCEL (*to the* DUC)

I think it's the most beautiful painting in the world.

Duc

I've probably seen it. But anyway, Charles (*he points to the painting on the wall*), what would you say this was?

Swann

A bad joke.

Duc

Oh, would you?

> *The* Duchesse *comes in. She wears a gown of red satin, the skirt bordered with spangles, an ostrich feather in her hair.*

Duchesse

Charles! Marcel! How delightful. What a pity we have to go out. Dining out is such a bore. There are evenings when one would sooner die. But perhaps dying is an even greater bore, who knows? (*She looks at* Swann's *hat.*) How nice to have one's hat lined with green leather. But with you, Charles, everything is always charming, whether it's what you wear or what you say, what you read or what you do. Which reminds me. We're thinking of spending next spring in Italy and Sicily. Will you come with us? It would make such a difference to us. I'm not thinking only of the pleasure of seeing you but of all the things you could explain to us there. Admit it. You know everything.

Swann

I'm afraid it won't be possible.

Duc

What a pity.

Duchesse

I'd like to know how, ten months before the time, you can know that a thing will be impossible.

Swann

I'm not very well.

DUCHESSE

Yes, you do look a little pale. But I'm asking you to come next year, not next week!

A FOOTMAN *enters.*

FOOTMAN

The carriage is at the door, Your Grace.

DUC

Come on, Oriane. We'll be late.

230. INT. THE GUERMANTES' HOUSE. THE STAIRS.

They all walk down the stairs.

DUCHESSE

Charles, give me in one word the reason you won't come to Italy.

SWANN (*gently*)

Because by next spring I shall have been dead for some time. According to the doctors I have only three or four months to live.

The FOOTMAN *opens the door. She pauses.*

DUCHESSE

What's that?

231. EXT. THE GUERMANTES' COURTYARD. THE CARRIAGE.

The DUCHESSE, SWANN, *and* MARCEL *on the steps.*
The DUC *at the carriage.*

DUCHESSE

You're joking.

SWANN

It would be a joke in charming taste. I'm sorry . . . but since you asked me . . . but you'll be late, I mustn't keep you.

DUCHESSE

Being late is not of any importance.

DUC

Oriane, you know perfectly well that Madame de Saint-Euverte insists on dining at eight o'clock sharp. I'm sorry, Charles, but it's ten to eight already and Oriane is notorious for being late.

DUCHESSE (*to* SWANN)

I can't believe what you're saying. But we must talk about it quietly. Come to luncheon, please, any day you like. And we'll talk.

She puts her foot on the step of the carriage.

DUC

Oriane, what on earth are you doing? You're wearing black shoes! With a red dress! Go upstairs and put some red ones on, for goodness' sake!

DUCHESSE

But you say we're late.

DUC

What does it matter whether we're late or not? Anyway we're not late. The point is you can't possibly go into that house in a red dress and black shoes.

The DUCHESSE *goes into the house.*

DUC (*to* SWANN *and* MARCEL)

A red dress with black shoes.

SWANN

I thought they went rather well together.

DUC

I don't say you're wrong, but it's really far preferable to match the dress, I'm quite convinced of that. I'm dying of hunger. I had a terrible lunch. As for you, Charles, don't believe a word those doctors tell you. You'll live to bury us all.

232. *MARCEL LOOKING AT SWANN.*

233. *SWANN LOOKS AT MARCEL, BRIEFLY.*

234. *INT. BALLROOM. BALBEC CASINO. 1901. (SILENT SHOT.)*

>Albertine *and* Andrée *dancing together.*

235. *INT. FOYER. GRAND HOTEL. BALBEC. 1901.*

>Marcel *(21) and the* Manager *are waiting for the lift.*

>Albertine*'s voice over:*

>>Albertine *(softly)*
>Oh, how heavenly.

236. *INT. MARCEL'S BEDROOM. BALBEC HOTEL. 1901. DAY. HIGH SHOT.*

>*The door shuts.* Marcel *is alone.*
>*He bends to unbutton his boots.*
>
>*He stops, suddenly rigid, remains bent.*

237. *C.U. MARCEL.*

>*His face, overcome with grief.*
>*On the soundtrack, three knocks are heard, on the wall.*

238. *INT. MARCEL'S HOTEL BEDROOM. THE FOLLOWING NIGHT.*

>Marcel, *in a dressing gown, sits still in a chair by the window.*
>
>*Dawn is growing over the sea.*
>
>*The bed is disturbed.*
>
>*He sits still.*

There is a soft knock at the door. He looks up.
The door opens. His MOTHER *comes in.*

Her hair, graying, is disheveled.
She wears GRANDMOTHER'S *dressing gown and for a moment is indistinguishable from her.*
MARCEL *stares at her in astonishment.*

> MOTHER
> Why are you looking at me like that? (*Gently.*) Ah. Yes. I look like your grandmother.

She goes towards him.

> MOTHER
> Why are you sitting in that chair? What's the matter? What is it?

She takes him in her arms. He weeps.

239. INT. MARCEL'S HOTEL BEDROOM. MORNING. THE DOOR.

> *The door opens.* FRANÇOISE.

> FRANÇOISE
> Mademoiselle Albertine is here to see you.

240. INT. THE ROOM.

> MARCEL *is at the window, looking out.*
> *Included in the shot is the framed photograph of* GRANDMOTHER, *standing on a cabinet.*
> *He turns.*

> FRANÇOISE
> Mademoiselle Albertine's here.

> MARCEL
> Tell her I can't see her.

> FRANÇOISE *goes out.*

> MARCEL *stares at the photograph.*

94

241. INT. HOTEL BEDROOM. DAY.

ALBERTINE *and* MARCEL *sitting.*

ALBERTINE

Would you like us to meet every day?

MARCEL

No. I can't. I don't feel ... very bright. But we'll see each other ... from time to time.

ALBERTINE

I'll come any time you want. I'll stay with you as long as you like.

242. INT. MARCEL'S HOTEL BEDROOM. ANOTHER DAY.

ALBERTINE, *in a different dress, on the bed in* MARCEL'*s arms.*

She looks at her watch, jumps up, goes to mirror, combs her hair.

ALBERTINE

I must go.

MARCEL

What? Why?

ALBERTINE

I have to be somewhere at five o'clock.

MARCEL

Where?

ALBERTINE

I have to pay a call on a friend of my aunt's. At Infreville.

MARCEL

But you didn't mention this when you came.

ALBERTINE

I didn't want to upset you. She's at home every day at five o'clock. I can't be late.

MARCEL

But if she's at home every day why do you have to go
today?

ALBERTINE

She expects me. My aunt expects me to go.

MARCEL

But what difference does a day make?

ALBERTINE

Well . . . as a matter of fact, I've arranged to meet some
of my girl friends there. It'll be less boring.

MARCEL

Oh. So you prefer this boring lady and your friends to
me?

ALBERTINE

I've said I'll give the girls a lift. Otherwise they can't get
back.

MARCEL

There are trains from Infreville up till ten o'clock at
night.

ALBERTINE

Yes, but she might ask them to stay for dinner.

Pause.

MARCEL

All right. Listen. I feel some fresh air will do me good.
I'll come with you, just for the ride. I won't come into
the house. I'll just go with you to the door.

ALBERTINE *stares at him, still.*

MARCEL

I really feel like some fresh air.

ALBERTINE

Let's go in the other direction. It's prettier.

MARCEL

The other direction? But you were going to see your
aunt's friend.

ALBERTINE

Oh, I can't be bothered.

MARCEL

Don't be silly. You must go. She's expecting you.

ALBERTINE

She won't notice whether I'm there or not. I can go
tomorrow, next week, the week after, it doesn't matter.

MARCEL

And your friends?

ALBERTINE

They can walk back. It'll do them good.

He studies her.

MARCEL

I'm not coming with you.

ALBERTINE

Why not?

MARCEL

You don't want me to come with you.

ALBERTINE

How can you say that?

MARCEL

Because you're a liar.

ALBERTINE

I am not! Really, it's too bad. I alter all my plans, so that
I can spend a nice long evening with you alone and all
you can do is insult me. You're cruel. I don't want to see
you again. Ever.

MARCEL

That would be wise.

ALBERTINE *looks at her watch.*

ALBERTINE

In that case I shall go to see my aunt's friend.

She leaves the room.

243. *EXT. PARIS STREET. NIGHT. 1880.*

> SWANN, *in foreground, looks towards* ODETTE's *house, which is dark and silent.*

244. *EXT. BALBEC BEACH. NIGHT. 1901.*

> *Moonlight. The camera moves through the dunes. Two shapes, lying in a dune, embracing.*

> ALBERTINE's VOICE

Oh my dear, my dear.

245. *EXT. PROMENADE. BALBEC. DAY. 1901.*

> MARCEL *walking towards the Casino.*
> DR. COTTARD *calls to him.*

> COTTARD

Hullo!

> MARCEL *stops.*

> COTTARD

You remember me? I'm Doctor Cottard. I treated your grandmother. To no avail, I'm afraid. Well, well.

> MARCEL (*shaking hands*)

Yes, of course.

> COTTARD

I'm just on my way to the Verdurins'. They've got a house for the summer near here. La Raspelière. Why don't you come with me? They'd be delighted to see you.

> MARCEL

I'm afraid I'm meeting some friends in the Casino.

> COTTARD

Ah. Well, I'll come in with you for a bit, if I may. My train is not till six.

> *They walk towards the Casino.*

> COTTARD

You must come to La Raspelière sometime soon. The

Verdurins have a remarkable position in society, you
know. They entertain all the very best people. Do you
know, they say Madame Verdurin is worth at least
thirty-five million? Thirty-five million, what do you
think of that? And of course she's done so much for the
arts, a very great deal. You're a writer yourself, aren't
you? That's why she'd be delighted to meet you.

246. *INT. CASINO. BALBEC. BALLROOM.*

There are no men in the room.
A few girls sit at tables, drinking. A girl is playing a
waltz on a piano. About half a dozen girls are
dancing together.

ALBERTINE *and* ANDRÉE *dance together.*

MARCEL *and* COTTARD *stand watching at the door.*

MARCEL

They dance well together, don't they? Girls?

COTTARD

Parents are very rash to allow their daughters to form
such habits. I'd never let mine come here. (*Indicating*
ALBERTINE *and* ANDRÉE.) Look at those two. It's not
sufficiently known that women derive most excitement
from their breasts. Theirs are completely touching. Look
at them.

ALBERTINE *and* ANDRÉE *dancing close together.*
ANDRÉE *whispers to* ALBERTINE. ALBERTINE *laughs.*
They ease the contact.

247. *INT. BALLROOM.*

MARCEL *sitting at a table with* ANDRÉE *by the*
mirrored wall. At the next table ALBERTINE, *with*
GISÈLE *and* ROSEMONDE. ALBERTINE *has her back to*
the room.

ANDRÉE *turns her head sharply as two women walk*
into the room and sit. MARCEL *follows her gaze.*

MARCEL

What are you looking at?

ANDRÉE

Those women.

MARCEL

Which?

ANDRÉE

Over there. Do you know who they are?

MARCEL

No.

ANDRÉE

Léa, the actress. And her friend. They live together quite openly. It's a scandal.

MARCEL

Oh ... You've no sympathy with that kind of thing, then?

ANDRÉE

Me? I loathe that kind of thing. I'm like Albertine in that. We both loathe that kind of thing.

LÉA *talks quietly to her friend, who listens gravely.*

248. *THE BACK OF ALBERTINE'S HEAD.*

GISÈLE *and* ROSEMONDE *whispering.*

In the mirror beyond them, ALBERTINE'*s face, glimpsed.*

249. *INT. MARCEL'S HOTEL. SITTING ROOM. DAY.*

MARCEL *and* ALBERTINE *enter the room.*
He closes the door. She speaks at once.

ALBERTINE

What have you got against me?

MARCEL *walks to the window, turns from it, sits, looks at her gravely.*

100

MARCEL
Do you really want me to tell you the truth?

ALBERTINE
Yes, I do.

He speaks quietly.

MARCEL
I admire Andrée ... greatly. I always have. There you are. That's the truth. You and I can be friends, I hope, but nothing more. Once, I was on the point of falling in love with you, but that time ... can't be recaptured. I'm sorry to be so frank. The truth is always unpleasant—for someone. I love Andrée.

ALBERTINE
I see. I don't mind your frankness. I see. But I'd just like to know what I've done.

MARCEL
Done? You haven't done anything. I've just explained to you—

ALBERTINE
Yes, I have. Or you think I have.

MARCEL
Why can't you listen?

ALBERTINE
Why can't you tell me?

Silence.

MARCEL
I've heard reports.

She gazes at him.

MARCEL
Reports ... about your way of life.

ALBERTINE
My way of life?

MARCEL

I have a profound disgust for women ... tainted with
that vice.

Pause.

MARCEL

You see, I have heard that your ... accomplice ... is
Andrée, and since Andrée is the woman I love, you can
understand my grief.

ALBERTINE *looks at him steadily.*

ALBERTINE

Who told you this rubbish?

MARCEL

I can't tell you.

ALBERTINE

Andrée and I both detest that sort of thing. We find it
revolting.

MARCEL

You're saying it's not true?

ALBERTINE

If it were true I would tell you. I would be quite honest
with you. Why not? But I'm telling you it's absolutely
untrue.

MARCEL

Do you swear it?

ALBERTINE

I swear it.

She walks to him and sits by him on the sofa.

ALBERTINE (*softly*)

I swear it.

She takes his hand.

ALBERTINE

You are silly.

She strokes his hand.

ALBERTINE

All those stories about Andrée . . .

She touches his face.

ALBERTINE

You are silly. I'm your Albertine.

She strokes his face.

ALBERTINE

Aren't you glad I'm here . . . sitting next to you?

MARCEL

Yes.

She attempts to kiss him. His mouth is shut.
She passes her tongue over his lips.

ALBERTINE

Open your mouth. Open your mouth, you great bear.

She forces his mouth open, kisses him, forcing him
down on the sofa.

250. *INT. ROOM IN SANATORIUM. 1917. DAY.*

MARCEL (37) *sitting at his desk, motionless as an owl.*
The desk is empty.
Over this shot GRANDMOTHER's *voice:*

GRANDMOTHER (V.O.)

How's your work getting on?

Pause.

GRANDMOTHER (V.O., *gently*)

Oh I'm sorry, I won't ask you again.

251. *EXT. BEACH. BALBEC. DAY. 1901.*

MARCEL *and* MOTHER *sitting in deck chairs.*

MOTHER

I think you should know that Albertine's aunt believes
you are going to marry Albertine.

MARCEL

Oh?

MOTHER

You're spending a great deal of money on her. They naturally think it would be a very good marriage, from her point of view.

Pause.

MARCEL

What do you think of her yourself?

MOTHER

Albertine? Well, it's not I that will be marrying her, is it? I don't think your grandmother would have liked me to influence you. But if she can make you happy . . .

MARCEL

She bores me. I have no intention of marrying her.

MOTHER

In that case I should see less of her.

252. EXT. DONCIÈRES STATION. PLATFORM. DAY.

SAINT-LOUP (23) *is standing on the platform.*
He is dressed in uniform and has with him a small dog, on a leash.

The little train draws in.
MARCEL, *leaning out of a carriage, waves.*

The train stops. MARCEL *jumps out. They shake hands.*

SAINT-LOUP

I just got your telegram. Good to see you.

MARCEL

I thought it might be nice to meet, if only for five minutes.

SAINT-LOUP

Brilliant idea!

MARCEL (*turning to carriage*)

Albertine, come out and meet Robert.

ALBERTINE *steps down from the train.*

MARCEL

Mademoiselle Albertine Simonet. The Marquis de
Saint-Loup.

SAINT-LOUP *bows.*

ALBERTINE

Oh, what a lovely little dog. What's his name?

SAINT-LOUP

She's a bitch. Pepi.

ALBERTINE

Hullo, Pepi.

MARCEL

We're on our way to the Verdurins'. Pity you can't
come with us.

SAINT-LOUP

I'm afraid even if I could I wouldn't. I find that sort of
atmosphere maddening.

ALBERTINE *is playing with the dog.*
The leash tightens about SAINT-LOUP*'s legs.*
ALBERTINE*'s body brushes against* SAINT-LOUP.

ALBERTINE

Sorry! Your dog is so enchanting. Come here, Pepi.

MARCEL

What do you mean?

ALBERTINE

Look! Your little dog has left hairs on your lovely
uniform. Isn't that terrible? Look at your leg. You
naughty little dog!

SAINT-LOUP

They'll brush off. (*To* MARCEL.) They're a sect. (*With a
smile.*) A naughty little sect. They're all butter to those

who belong, contemptuous of those who don't. They're not for me.

STATION MASTER *blows his whistle.*

MARCEL

We must get in.

ALBERTINE

Good-bye, little dog. What did you say her name was?

SAINT-LOUP

Pepi.

They all shake hands.

253. *EXT. ROAD TO LA RASPELIÈRE.*

CHARLUS *and* MOREL *in a chauffeur-driven car. They sit expressionless.*

MOREL *is twenty-one, very handsome.*

254. *INT. THE DRAWING ROOM. LA RASPELIÈRE. SUNSET.*

The drawing room is very large. Displays of fresh grasses, poppies, wild flowers alternate with a similar theme painted on the walls. Huge windows look down over the terraces.

MME. VERDURIN

We have a really brilliant musician coming tonight. My husband and I discovered him. His name's Morel. He has a great future. Unfortunately an old friend of his family has apparently latched on to him. So we'll have to put up with him. Someone called the Baron de Charlus.

MME. VERDURIN (59) *turns to join a group consisting of the* MARQUIS *and* MARQUISE DE CAMBREMER, MME. COTTARD, M. VERDURIN, *and* ALBERTINE.

ALBERTINE *is exquisitely dressed.*

106

BRICHOT (64), COTTARD (57), *and* MARCEL *stand apart.*

BRICHOT *is half blind.*

BRICHOT (*to* COTTARD)

By the way, did you hear the news? Dechambre's dead.

COTTARD

That's right. He is. Liver. (*To* MARCEL.) Dechambre was Madame Verdurin's favorite pianist. Quite a young man too.

BRICHOT

Not as young as all that. He used to play Vinteuil's sonata for Swann, years ago, don't you remember?

COTTARD

Did he? I can't remember that.

BRICHOT

Poor Swann.

COTTARD

What's the matter with Swann?

BRICHOT

He's dead, my dear fellow. He died about two months ago.

COTTARD

Did he really? Nobody told me. My goodness, they're all dying like flies.

M. VERDURIN (61) *joins them.*

BRICHOT (*to* M. VERDURIN)

Terrible news about Dechambre.

M. VERDURIN

Yes, but it's no use crying over spilt milk; talking about him won't bring him back to life, will it? And for heaven's sake don't start talking about Dechambre to Madame Verdurin. She's quite morbidly sensitive. When she heard he was dead she almost cried.

107

COTTARD

Did she really?

COTTARD *looks across to the* CAMBREMERS.

COTTARD (*to* M. VERDURIN)

Did you say those two were a marquis and marquise?

M. VERDURIN

Yes, yes, what does it matter? (*To* MARCEL.) We've rented this house from them for the summer. They're ghastly bores, but we had to invite them once. Courtesy.

COTTARD (*murmuring*)

A marquis and marquise. (*To* MARCEL.) Would you believe it? You meet everyone here, you know.

A FOOTMAN *opens the door.*

FOOTMAN

Monsieur Morel and the Baron de Charlus.

The VERDURINS *walk towards* MOREL *and* CHARLUS.

MARCEL *and* MOREL *catch each other's eye.*
A flash of recognition.

255. *ALBERTINE ALONE BY THE WINDOWS.*

In background at the far end of the room MOREL *is introducing the* VERDURINS *to* CHARLUS.

ALBERTINE *is looking at* MOREL.
She turns away to gaze out of the window.

256. *AT THE DOOR OF THE DINING ROOM.*

MME. VERDURIN *whispering to her husband.*

MME. VERDURIN

Shall I offer my arm to the Baron?

M. VERDURIN

No, surely not? Cambremer is a marquis, Charlus a baron. A marquis is higher than a baron. Isn't it? Anyway, I'm sure I'm right. Cambremer must be on your right at the table. Go in with him.

257. INT. DINING ROOM.

From the dining table the camera sees MME. VER-
DURIN *on the arm of the* MARQUIS DE CAMBREMER
(55) lead the procession into the room.
A great fish sits on the sideboard. M. DE CAMBREMER
stares at it as he passes.

M. DE CAMBREMER
I say, that looks a fine animal.

The guests take their places.
MME. VERDURIN *sits at the head of the table,* M. DE
CAMBREMER *to her right,* MARCEL *to her left.*
To MARCEL's *left,* MME. COTTARD, BRICHOT, MOREL,
and CHARLUS.
To M. DE CAMBREMER's *right,* ALBERTINE, COTTARD,
MME. DE CAMBREMER.
M. VERDURIN *at the foot of the table.*

M. DE CAMBREMER (*to* MME. VERDURIN)
I feel so at home here, you know.

MME. VERDURIN
You must notice a good many changes, I should think.
There were some horrid little plush chairs in this room,
which I must confess I packed off at once to the attic—

*She picks up a piece of bread, bites into it, and
mutters into her bread:*

MME. VERDURIN
—even that's too good for them.

258. MME. DE CAMBREMER (50), HEARING THIS RE-
MARK, STIFFENS.

She is very plump.

COTTARD (*to* MME. DE CAMBREMER)
Fine house, this, don't you think?

MME. DE CAMBREMER
We own it.

109

259. *MOREL LOOKING ACROSS THE TABLE AT ALBERTINE.*

260. *ALBERTINE LOOKING ACROSS THE TABLE AT MOREL.*

261. *MARCEL LOOKING AT ALBERTINE LOOKING AT MOREL.*

> COTTARD (*V.O., to* MARCEL)
> When you come to a relatively high altitude such as this, do you find the change increases your tendency to choking fits?

> MARCEL

No.

262. *THE TABLE.*

> *The fish is being served.*

> M. DE CAMBREMER (*turning*)
> Choking fits? Who has choking fits?

> MARCEL

I do. Sometimes.

> M. DE CAMBREMER

Really? Do you? You know, I can't tell you how amused I am to hear that. You see, my sister has them too. She's had choking fits for years. I must tell her I met a fellow sufferer. She'll be so amused.

263. *CHARLUS AND MOREL.*

> MOREL *is looking at* ALBERTINE.
> CHARLUS *is looking at* MOREL.

> M. VERDURIN (*V.O., to* CHARLUS, *whispering*)
> Of course, I realized from the first words we exchanged that you were one of us.

> CHARLUS *lifts his eyebrows, looks at* M. VERDURIN.

I beg your pardon?

264. M. VERDURIN AND CHARLUS.

VERDURIN

I mean, I can understand how little such things mean to
you.

CHARLUS

I don't quite follow you.

VERDURIN

I'm referring to the fact that we gave precedence to the
Marquis. That the Marquis is seated to Madam Verdurin's right. I myself attach no significance whatever to
titles of nobility, but of course you do understand that
as Monsieur Cambremer is a marquis and you are only a
baron—

CHARLUS

Pardon me. I am also Duc de Brabant, Damoiseau de
Montargis, Prince d'Oléron, de Carency, de Viareggio,
and des Dunes. However, please do not distress yourself.
It is not of the slightest importance, here.

265. INT. DRAWING ROOM. AFTER DINNER.

The CAMBREMERS *whispering.*

MME. DE CAMBREMER

They've destroyed the house, totally desecrated it. But
I'm not in the least surprised. You can't expect good
taste from retired tradespeople, which is what I would
say they are.

M. DE CAMBREMER

I quite like the chandeliers.

MME. DE CAMBREMER

I think we should put up the rent.

266. *INT. DRAWING ROOM.*

>
> Morel *playing the violin, accompanied by* Charlus
> *on the piano.*
> *The music stops. Calls of "Sublime!" etc.*
> Mme. Cottard (53) *is asleep in a chair.*
>
> Charlus *turns to* Marcel.
>
> > CHARLUS
> > He plays like a god, don't you think?
>
> > Mme. Verdurin (*to* Morel)
> > Please let us have some more.
>
> > MOREL
> > No, sorry. I have to go soon.

267. *C.U. ALBERTINE, SITTING.*

268. *THE ROOM.*

> > COTTARD (*to* Mme. Cottard)
> > Léontine, you're snoring.
>
> > Mme. Cottard (*faintly*)
> > I am listening to Monsieur Swann, my dear.
>
> > Mme. Verdurin
> > She's in touch with spirits, doctor, and rather dubious
> > spirits at that.
>
> > COTTARD
> > Swann! (*He shouts.*) Léontine! Pull yourself together!
>
> > Mme. Cottard (*murmuring*)
> > My bath is nice and hot. (*She sits up abruptly.*) Oh good
> > lord, what is it, what have I been saying, I was thinking
> > about my hat, in another minute I should have been
> > asleep, it's that wretched fire.
>
> > COTTARD (*shouting*)
> > There's no fire in sight! We're in the middle of summer.
> > (*To the gathering.*) She looks like an old beetroot!

269. *MOREL SIPPING A DRINK.*

> *He is sitting in a chair next to* ALBERTINE.
> *They are looking in different directions.*

270. THE ROOM.

> CHARLUS *and* MARCEL *are looking towards* MOREL.

CHARLUS

I shall make him great.

> MME. VERDURIN *approaches* MOREL.

MME. VERDURIN

My Mozart! My young Mozart! Would you like to stay
the night? We have some lovely rooms facing the sea.

CHARLUS (*moving to her*)

Impossible. He must get back to his own bed like a good
little boy, obedient and well behaved.

> MME. VERDURIN *looks down at* ALBERTINE.

MME. VERDURIN

What a pretty dress you're wearing.

ALBERTINE

Thank you, madame.

MME. VERDURIN

Would you like to stay the night? I can show you a room
I think you'd adore.

MARCEL (*moving forward*)

I'm afraid it's not possible. Mademoiselle Simonet's
aunt is expecting her.

MME. VERDURIN

What a pity.

271. *EXT. LA RASPELIÈRE. CLIFF TOP. NIGHT.*

> *Sound of the sea.*
> *In the distance the lights of the house.*

The door is open. The carriages are being brought to the front of the house.

The guests stand in the moonlight. Their distant voices.

Sound of the sea.

272. EXT. THE HOUSE.

> CHARLUS *is talking to the* VERDURINS *and* MME. DE CAMBREMER.
>
> MARCEL *stands with* ALBERTINE, MOREL *in background, his back to them.*
>
> M. DE CAMBREMER *turns to* MARCEL.

M. DE CAMBREMER

You must come to see us soon. You could discuss your attacks with my sister. I'm sure she'll be most amused.

273. INT. CARRIAGE. THE LITTLE TRAIN FROM LA RASPELIÈRE. NIGHT.

> MARCEL *and* ALBERTINE *alone.*

ALBERTINE (yawning)

What a lovely house. I really did enjoy myself.

MARCEL

A waste of time.

ALBERTINE

I had a lovely time.

> *Pause.*

MARCEL

What did you think of Morel's playing?

ALBERTINE

Oh . . . he's a beautiful player.

MARCEL (sharply)

His father was my uncle's valet.

ALBERTINE

Was he? Well, he's a beautiful player.

How could you behave so disgracefully with Saint-Loup?

ALBERTINE
Saint-Loup? What do you mean?

MARCEL
Rubbing against him, flirting with him. What did you think you were doing.?

ALBERTINE
Oh, I did that deliberately. I didn't want to give him the impression that you and I were ... close friends. But anyway, I wasn't flirting with him, I was flirting with his dog.

MARCEL
Didn't you hear him say? The dog was a bitch.

ALBERTINE
Oh.

Silence.

ALBERTINE *looks out of the window.*

MARCEL
I must finish with all this. I must have done with it.

He looks at the back of ALBERTINE's *head and mutters:*

MARCEL
Waste of time.

Pause.

MARCEL
For instance, there was one thing I did want to ask them, but of course one never gets the chance.

ALBERTINE
What?

MARCEL
You wouldn't be interested.

Slight pause.

MARCEL

About a composer. Used to be a protégé of theirs. He
wrote a sonata. I want to find out if he's written
anything else.

ALBERTINE

What composer?

MARCEL

If I told you his name was Vinteuil, would you be any
the wiser?

ALBERTINE

Vinteuil? How funny.

He looks at her.

ALBERTINE

Do you remember once I told you I had a friend, older
than me, who has been a sister, a mother to me, with
whom I spent the happiest years of my life, at Trieste?

MARCEL (*slowly*)

No. I don't remember.

ALBERTINE

Oh yes. In fact I'm to join her in a few weeks at
Cherbourg, we're going on a cruise together. Well, this
woman is the dearest, most intimate friend of Vinteuil's
daughter. In fact, I know Vinteuil's daughter almost as
well as I know her friend. I always call them my two big
sisters.

MARCEL *does not comment. The train runs on.*
Silence.

274. *INT. MARCEL'S ROOM. HOTEL.*

MOTHER *sitting.* MARCEL *standing.*

MARCEL

I know what I'm going to say will distress you. I must go
back to Paris. I want to take Albertine with me, to stay,
as my guest, in our flat. It is absolutely necessary—and

116

please don't let's argue about it, because I am quite clear in my own mind, and because I shan't change my mind again, and because otherwise I couldn't go on living—it is absolutely necessary that I marry Albertine.

275. *MOTHER'S FACE.*

276. *MLLE. VINTEUIL RUNNING TO THE WINDOW TO CLOSE SHUTTERS.*

277. *ODETTE PLAYING VINTEUIL'S SONATA. SWANN LISTENING.*

278. *EXT. FIELD. DAY.*
> *A riderless horse gallops away from the camera.*

279. *INT. LIBRARY. MARCEL'S PARIS FLAT. NIGHT. 1902.*
> *Tapestries hang on the walls.*
> ALBERTINE *is asleep in bed.*
> MARCEL *stands watching her.*

280. *INT. KITCHEN.*
> *A bunch of syringa lying on the kitchen table.*

281. *INT. THE LIBRARY. (ALBERTINE'S ROOM.) NIGHT.*
> ALBERTINE, *in nightdress, standing at the open window.*

282. *INT. MARCEL'S FLAT. CORRIDOR. MORNING.*
> FRANÇOISE *walking along corridor with tray.*
> *She stops at library door and knocks.*

FRANÇOISE
Mademoiselle Simonet, your coffee.

117

283.   *INT. TWO ADJOINING BATHROOMS.*

>   *Frosted glass.*
>   *The shape of* ALBERTINE *seen through the glass drying herself.*
>   *She is humming.*
>
>   MARCEL *in other bathroom listening.*
>   *He smiles.*

284.   *INT. MARCEL'S ROOM. MORNING.*

>   *He is in bed.* ALBERTINE *enters.*

ALBERTINE

Good morning.

>   *She gets on the bed. They kiss.*

ALBERTINE

What lovely skin. You've shaved.

MARCEL

I did, yes—then got back into bed.

ALBERTINE

You're lazy. Did you sleep badly?

MARCEL

Very.

ALBERTINE

Are you feeling ill?

MARCEL

No. But not well either. I'll stay in bed today.

ALBERTINE

My poor boy.

MARCEL

Andrée will be here soon, won't she, to take you out?

ALBERTINE

Yes.

MARCEL

Where will you go?

ALBERTINE

Oh, I don't know. Why don't you come with us? Or I can tell her to go home and we can go out by ourselves.

MARCEL

Andrée is a very good friend . . . to both of us.

ALBERTINE

I didn't say she wasn't.

MARCEL

I trust her.

Pause.

MARCEL

Anyway I'm not well enough to go out.

ALBERTINE

Will you work then, if we leave you alone? Will you try?

MARCEL

Yes, yes.

ALBERTINE

I'll bring you paper and pencils and put them on the bed for you, so you won't have to get up. Or if you like, I'll stay here with you.

MARCEL

How can I work if you're with me?

ALBERTINE

Would I distract you?

She laughs.

ALBERTINE

Sometimes I feel I never want to go out at all, never want to leave you. Never.

She nuzzles him.

ALBERTINE

But if you ever want me to go you'll tell me, won't you? You'll tell me quite simply? And I'll go.

He stares at her uncertainly. She smiles.

ALBERTINE

That is, if your parents don't ask me to go first.

MARCEL

My parents are perfectly happy for you to stay here, as my friend. They don't mind your staying here . . . at all.

ALBERTINE

I don't mind either.

MARCEL

I might even marry you.

ALBERTINE

No, no. There are so many other prettier, more intelligent girls than me . . . for you.

The doorbell rings.

ALBERTINE

That's Andrée.

285. *INT. ALBERTINE'S BEDROOM. EVENING. (SAME AS SHOT NO. 279.)*

ALBERTINE *sleeping on the bed.*

MARCEL *watches her.*

He gets on to the bed and lies behind her, very close.

286. *THEIR HEADS.*

ALBERTINE, *eyes closed. Her eyelids flutter.*

MARCEL, *eyes open, moving gently against her.*

287. *INT. MARCEL'S ROOM. AFTERNOON.*

The door is open. Through the door we see ALBERTINE *and* ANDRÉE *walking down the corridor.* ALBERTINE *goes into her room.*

ANDRÉE *enters* MARCEL'S *room, closes the door.*

A pile of notebooks lies unopened on the bed.

ANDRÉE

We had a very pleasant time.

MARCEL

Where did you go?

ANDRÉE

Versailles.

MARCEL

Did you meet anyone?

ANDRÉE

Albertine met an old friend.

MARCEL

Who?

ANDRÉE

An old school friend. I can't remember her name.

MARCEL

What was she like?

ANDRÉE

Mousy. Rather plain, actually.

MARCEL

What did they talk about?

ANDRÉE

Paintings. All rather schoolgirlish.

Pause.

MARCEL

And that's all?

ANDRÉE

Absolutely.

288. *ALBERTINE IN BED, LOOKING UP, HAIR OVER PILLOW.*

ALBERTINE

I was so ignorant before I met you, wasn't I? I'm really quite intelligent now. Aren't I? It's all due to you. I owe everything to you.

289. *VIEW OF COURTYARD FROM WINDOW OF AL-BERTINE'S ROOM. DAY.*

> MARCEL *walking across courtyard with a bunch of syringa.*
>
> *Sharp sound of sudden movement in room. Rustle of skirt.*

290. *INT. STAIRWAY.*

> MARCEL *climbing stairs, carrying flowers. He looks up.*
>
> ANDRÉE *comes out of the door of the flat.*

MARCEL

What, are you back already?

ANDRÉE

We've just got in. Albertine wanted to write a letter, so I've left her alone.

MARCEL

A letter? To whom?

ANDRÉE

Her aunt.

MARCEL

A pity you've closed the door. I've forgotten my key. Is Françoise in?

ANDRÉE

She's out shopping. That's syringa, isn't it?

MARCEL

Yes.

ANDRÉE

Albertine hates syringa. It's the scent, it's so strong.

MARCEL

Does she? I didn't know that.

ANDRÉE

The scent is overpowering. Well, good-bye.

122

She descends.
MARCEL *rings the bell.*
The door is opened immediately, by ALBERTINE.
The hall is dark.

ALBERTINE

Syringa! Oh!

She runs down the hall.

MARCEL

I'll take them into the kitchen.

291. INT. KITCHEN.

MARCEL *puts syringa on table, goes back into hall.*

ALBERTINE'S VOICE

I'm in your room.

He goes in.

292. INT. MARCEL'S BEDROOM.

She is lying on the bed.

MARCEL

I'm sorry. I didn't realize you hated syringa.

ALBERTINE

It's their scent, that's all. It's so strong. It's probably all
over you. Don't come too near me until it wears off.

293. INT. MARCEL'S ROOM. MORNING.

He is in bed. FRANÇOISE *with coffee. She gives it to
him, stands, mutters.*

MARCEL

What?

She moves about the room, tidying.

FRANÇOISE

She'll land you in trouble, that one.

What do you mean?

FRANÇOISE

I've been with your family forty years.

MARCEL

What are you talking about?

FRANÇOISE

You're breaking your parents' hearts.

MARCEL

How dare you? My parents are perfectly happy, perfectly happy. My mother says so in all her letters.

FRANÇOISE

You are bringing this house into dangerous disrepute.

MARCEL

That's enough!

294. *INT. ALBERTINE'S ROOM. NIGHT.*

> ALBERTINE *is sleeping, murmuring.*
> MARCEL, *beside her, strains to catch the words.*

ALBERTINE

Oh, darling.

> *He frowns.*

295. *INT. SITTING ROOM. EVENING.*

> MARCEL *is looking at* ALBERTINE's *sketches.*

MARCEL

They're excellent.

ALBERTINE

They're not, no. If only I'd had drawing lessons.

> *He looks at her.*

MARCEL

You had drawing lessons, at Balbec.

Did I?

MARCEL

One evening. You couldn't see me. You said you had a drawing lesson.

ALBERTINE

Oh, so I did. She was such a bad teacher I'd forgotten all about it. She was hopeless.

Pause.

MARCEL

Oh, I've been meaning to ask you something—not that it's of the slightest importance . . .

ALBERTINE

What?

MARCEL

Have you ever met Léa?

ALBERTINE

Léa?

MARCEL

The actress.

ALBERTINE

No, I don't think so. Why?

MARCEL

What do you know about her? What kind of woman is she?

ALBERTINE

Perfectly respectable, as far as I know.

MARCEL

That's not what I've been led to understand.

ALBERTINE

I know nothing about it.

Pause.

MARCEL

You don't trust me, do you? Why? You know I love
you.

ALBERTINE

I trust only you. You know that. And you know I love
you.

Pause.

MARCEL

I've decided it's too dangerous for you to go riding. You
could easily have an accident.

She looks at him with a slight smile.

ALBERTINE

If I died, would you commit suicide?

296. INT. MARCEL'S BEDROOM. NIGHT.

*ALBERTINE in dressing gown. MARCEL takes off her
gown, opens her nightdress, looks at her breasts,
bends to take off her shoes.*
Smiling, she helps him take off her nightdress.
Briefly, we glimpse her naked body.
She lies on the bed.

297. C.U. ALBERTINE'S HEAD AND SHOULDERS.

Her arms are folded behind her head.

298. C.U. MARCEL LOOKING DOWN AT HER.

MARCEL *(softly)*

Oh darling.

299. INT. ALBERTINE'S BEDROOM. NIGHT. (SAME AS
SHOT NO. 281.)

ALBERTINE in nightdress standing by open window.

300. *INT. SITTING ROOM. MORNING.*

MARCEL *and* ALBERTINE *at window.*
Street cries of traders.

ALBERTINE

Oh listen! Those cries! Aren't they wonderful! Oysters! I've been longing for oysters! Mussels! I must have some mussels.

MARCEL

If they're not as fresh as the ones at Balbec, they'd make you very ill.

ALBERTINE

Listen! Onions, cabbages, carrots, oranges, all the things I want to eat. Françoise can cook us a dish of creamed carrots, can't she, with onion? We'll be eating all the sounds we hear, won't we, all the sounds will be sitting on a plate. Will you tell her?

MARCEL

Yes, yes.

ALBERTINE

I'd also like an ice, from Rebattets. I might look in and buy one.

MARCEL

You don't need to go to Rebattets. I can order one for you from the Ritz.

Pause.

ALBERTINE

Why? Are you going out?

MARCEL

I may, I may not.

Pause.

ALBERTINE

Well, if you do order me an ice, I'd like one of those old-fashioned ones, the ones that are shaped like temples, churches, things like that, monuments. A raspberry or vanilla monument. I shall make its pink granite crumble and melt deep down in my throat. Isn't that well put? My lips will destroy pillar after pillar. Venetian strawberry churches will be demolished by my tongue. I'll swallow them up, so cool, cool, cool.

301. *INT. THE CORRIDOR. NIGHT.*

> *The corridor is dark.*
>
> Marcel's *door opens. He walks up the corridor to the door of* Albertine's *room. He stands still, listening.*
>
> *Silence.*

302. *EXT. BALBEC BEACH. DAY.*

> Albertine *outlined against the sea and sky, laughing.*

303. *INT. SITTING ROOM. EVENING.*

> Marcel *and* Albertine *at the table with coffee. Silence.*

MARCEL

You seem depressed.

ALBERTINE

I couldn't be happier.

MARCEL

You don't feel imprisoned?

ALBERTINE

I told you, I couldn't be happier.

> *Pause*

ALBERTINE

I might possibly look in at the Verdurins' tomorrow. I don't really want to, but I might.

MARCEL

Why?

ALBERTINE

I told you Andrée and I met Madame Verdurin by accident the other day, didn't I?

MARCEL

No. You didn't.

ALBERTINE

Didn't I? I thought I had. Anyway, she insisted that I go to see them one day for tea. I don't really want to, but I suppose it would be a change. She asked Andrée too.

304. *INT. MARCEL'S ROOM. EVENING.*

MARCEL *on telephone.*

MARCEL

Andrée.

ANDRÉE'S VOICE

Oh. Hullo.

MARCEL

You and Albertine are supposed to go to the Verdurins' tomorrow afternoon?

ANDRÉE

That's right.

MARCEL

Why?

ANDRÉE

Why?

MARCEL

Why does she want to go there?

ANDRÉE

Madame Verdurin asked us for tea, that's all. It's quite innocent.

MARCEL

Are you sure—

> FRANÇOISE *comes in, opens a drawer, puts some shirts in.*
> *He waits.*

ANDRÉE

Hullo?

MARCEL

Yes . . . yes . . . I'm sorry . . .

> FRANÇOISE *goes out.*

MARCEL

Are you sure there won't be someone there she wants to meet?

ANDRÉE

I can't think who.

MARCEL

I may come with you.

> *Pause.*

ANDRÉE

Ah.

305. *INT. ALBERTINE'S ROOM. EVENING.*

> MARCEL *enters.*

MARCEL

I may come with you.

ALBERTINE

Where?

MARCEL

To the Verdurins'. Tomorrow. For tea.

ALBERTINE

Oh. Yes, why not, if you'd like to. There's an awful mist about today, though. It'll probably clear by tomorrow. It would be so much nicer if you were there, of course. But I don't think I'll go, actually. I must get a white scarf to wear with this dress. I'll probably do that instead.

306. INT. SITTING ROOM. FOLLOWING EVENING.

> Marcel *and* Albertine *with coffee.*
> *Silence.*

MARCEL

Did you find the scarf you wanted?

ALBERTINE

No.

> *Pause.*

MARCEL

I'm feeling better tonight. I think I'll look in at the Guermantes', or Madame de Villeparisis's. I haven't been out for ages. Would you like to come?

ALBERTINE

No, thanks. My hair's all wrong today.

> *He goes to the door.*

MARCEL

Well, I'll have a little walk. You'll be here when I come back?

> *She looks at him.*

ALBERTINE

Of course.

307. MOREL TUNING HIS VIOLIN.

308. CHARLUS GREETING GUESTS.

309. THE VERDURINS STANDING GRIMLY.

310. EXT. STREET. EVENING. LONG SHOT.

> MARCEL, *walking in the distance.*
> *He is hailed and joined by* CHARLUS.
> *They walk along together.*
>
> *Over this:*

ALBERTINE

I might possibly look in at the Verdurins' tomorrow. I don't really want to, but I might.

311. *CHARLUS AND MARCEL WALKING. TWO SHOT.*

CHARLUS

I assure you, tonight will prove to be a quite memorable and even historic occasion. Do you know what you're in for?

MARCEL

No. What?

CHARLUS

The first performance of a new work by Vinteuil, played by Morel. I'm delighted you're coming. I would naturally have sent you an invitation but I understood you were ill. Are you better?

MARCEL

Thank you, yes. A new work? By Vinteuil?

CHARLUS

Yes, a septet.

MARCEL

But he's been dead for years.

CHARLUS

Indeed. But it transpires that he left illegible, quite indecipherable manuscripts everywhere, no more than scribblings. And can you guess who has been working on them, for years, trying to make sense of them? Mademoiselle Vinteuil's infamous friend, with his

132

daughter at her side. First they kill him by their shamelessness and now they insist on saving his work and thereby keeping him alive. It's a superb work and Morel will play it superbly. I believe the two disreputable ladies were at the rehearsal this afternoon. Morel said they were expected.

The camera pans to Marcel *and remains on him for the rest of* Charlus's *speech.*

CHARLUS

I haven't seen the rascal since this morning, when he came into my room and tried to pull me out of bed. Pure wickedness. He knows how I hate being seen first thing in the morning. After all, I'm no longer five and twenty, they won't choose me to be Queen of the May, will they? But I must confess the boy seems to grow more beautiful every day, wicked or not.

MARCEL

Mademoiselle Vinteuil, and her friend ... were expected at the Verdurins' this afternoon?

CHARLUS

They were expected.

He stops.

CHARLUS

I shall confide something to you. You are a writer—

MARCEL

No I'm not—

CHARLUS

You will be. You wish to be. You are interested therefore in the complex and mysterious tissues of human nature. Also I trust you, I've no idea why. I happened, by accident, you see, to open a letter addressed to Morel the other day. It was from the actress Léa, who as all the world knows, is a particularly notorious lesbian. Its indelicacy prevents me from repeating it in full, but it contained phrases—to Morel, remember—such as "You naughty little girl" and "Of course you're one of us, you pretty sweetheart." And the letter also made quite clear that other women, friends of Léa's, were most attracted to Morel. Lesbians, the lot of them. Now I have always known that Morel was "one of us." Oh, he's had women, women by the mile, he has women now, when he feels like it, and I couldn't care less, but these are not women. Do you follow me? When Léa refers to him as "one of us," what can she possibly mean? I thought he was one of *us*. I mean we know that Morel is——ambidextrous. Do you think he is also a lesbian?

MARCEL

I don't know.

CHARLUS (*wickedly*)

I mean, how on earth can a man be a lesbian? In other words, what do they *do?*

MARCEL

I don't know.

CHARLUS

I'm not surprised you can't help me. You are totally inexperienced in these matters.

CHARLUS *moves on, followed by* MARCEL.

CHARLUS

Have you heard that my nephew, Saint-Loup, is to marry Swann's daughter, Gilberte? A match that would have pleased Swann greatly, had he been alive to witness it, poor man.

They reach the door of the VERDURINS' *house.*

CHARLUS

I must tell you that I have issued the invitations for tonight myself. Madame Verdurin can ask her grocer and milliner and butcher acquaintances, not to mention the lavatory woman from the Champs-Élysées, to the next party. Tonight the cream of society will hear Morel play.

He looks sharply at MARCEL.

CHARLUS

What's the matter with you? You look ill. Are you feeling ill?

MARCEL

No. I'm perfectly all right.

They go into the house.
The camera holds on the door closing.

ALBERTINE (V.O.)

I don't really want to, but I might.

312. *INT. CONCERT ROOM. THE VERDURINS' HOUSE. EVENING.*

The VERDURINS *standing alone, their faces grim.*

In background CHARLUS *is welcoming the guests.*

The guests approach CHARLUS *immediately on entering the room. They ignore the* VERDURINS.

DUCHESSE DE GUERMANTES

Mémé, how lovely to see you. We do find you in the most unlikely houses these days. Where is this Mother Verdurin? I don't need to speak to her, do I?

313. *THE VERDURINS.*

MME. VERDURIN

I am the hostess. This is my house. He seems to have forgotten that. I will not stand for it.

The voice of the DUCHESSE *floats over.*

DUCHESSE

I do hope she won't put my name in the newspapers tomorrow. Nobody will ever speak to me again.

135

*Laughter from the gathering and further greetings
from and to* CHARLUS.

MARCEL *approaches the* VERDURINS.

MARCEL

Excuse me, isn't Mademoiselle Vinteuil supposed to be
here? With one of her friends?

In background the QUEEN OF NAPLES *approaches*
CHARLUS.
Other guests curtsey and bow to her.
She is sixty.

MME. VERDURIN

She sent a telegram. They were obliged to remain in the
country. (*To M.* VERDURIN.) Morel must know the truth
about that man. We owe it to him. You must speak to
him. He must be warned. It is our duty.

VERDURIN

I agree. But after the performance.

MME. VERDURIN

I have devoted my life to art, to music. We must save
him from that monster.

MARCEL (*to* MME. VERDURIN)

Will the actress Léa be here tonight, by any chance?

She looks at him sharply.

MME. VERDURIN

Certainly not!

314. *THE QUEEN OF NAPLES WITH CHARLUS.*

QUEEN OF NAPLES

May I meet our hostess?

CHARLUS

Our hostess! But of course, of course. Madame
Verdurin!

He moves to her.

CHARLUS

Her Majesty the Queen of Naples desires me to present you to her.

MME. VERDURIN

Oh!

CHARLUS *leads the* VERDURINS *to the* QUEEN.

CHARLUS

May I have the honor, Ma'am, to present Madame Verdurin, our hostess this evening. Monsieur Verdurin.

The VERDURINS *curtsey and bow, murmuring, "Your Majesty."*

QUEEN OF NAPLES

It is so kind of you to invite me to your beautiful house and on such an auspicious occasion. I am quite delighted to meet you.

MME. VERDURIN

You overwhelm me, Ma'am. I hope you may enjoy your visit to my temple of music, as I venture to call it.

QUEEN OF NAPLES

It is such a very pretty temple.

The musicians have mounted the platform and are tuning their instruments.
CHARLUS coughs loudly at the assembly, who take their seats. He leads the QUEEN to a chair.

MME. VERDURIN (*to* VERDURIN)

How simple and unaffected! That's the true blood royal. What a difference from the rest of these upstarts. I expect, if the truth were known, half these precious duchesses are on the books of the police.

The musicians are silent, about to begin.

The music begins.

The camera moves along the seated gathering.
Ladies nod their heads vacantly in supposed time to

137

the music. *Others turn to look at others, greeting them with smiles and waves. Others use their fans constantly.*

A Man *whispers to a* Lady.

Man

I keep forgetting the name of this composer. Who is it?

Charlus

Ssshh!

315. *MARCEL, LISTENING.*

> *Over all shots of* Marcel *the music is quite clear, pure, no extraneous sounds.*
>
> *His face is revitalized, unanxious, totally concentrated.*

316. THE AUDIENCE.

> *In all shots of the audience at this stage, the sound of the music is dominated by those of fans, feet shifting, yawns, coughs, and these sounds are at the forefront over shots of* Charlus, *sitting tensely, trying to concentrate, glancing furiously at the audience;* Mme. Verdurin, *sitting stiffly; the* Queen of Naples, *listening intently.*

317. MOREL PLAYING.

> *A lock of hair falls onto his forehead.*

318. *MARCEL, LISTENING.*

> (Note: *The septet continues over the following shots, which are now all silent, the music quite pure, no extraneous sounds.*
>
> *During the course of this sequence, the music will cross-fade to the climax of the third movement of the septet.*)

138

319. *MARCEL.*

320. *THE MUSICIANS.*

321. *THE AUDIENCE.*

322. *MARCEL.*

323. *YELLOW SCREEN.*

324. *THE MUSICIANS.*

325. *THE AUDIENCE.*

326. *MARCEL.*

327. *YELLOW SCREEN.*
    > *In this shot of the yellow screen the music reaches its sustained climax.*

328. *MARCEL.*
    > *Applause around him.*
    > *He sits still, joyous.*

329. *FLASH OF THE STEEPLES AT MARTINVILLE. SILENT.*

330. *M. VINTEUIL WALKING TOWARD CAMERA. SILENT.*
    > *In background* MLLE. VINTEUIL *and* FRIEND *playing the piano.*

331. *INT. CONCERT ROOM.*
    > *A queue of guests waits to speak to* CHARLUS.
    > *The* VERDURINS *stand apart, with* BRICHOT.

Two Ladies *are looking at some Impressionist paintings.*

Lady

What ghastly paintings.

The Duchesse de Guermantes *with* Charlus.

Duchesse

Honestly, Mémé, you are remarkable. If you were to stage an opera in a stable or bathroom it would still be perfectly charming.

Laughter.

Duchesse

Has there ever been a *Monsieur* Verdurin, by the way?

332. *THE VERDURINS WITH BRICHOT.*

Mme. Verdurin

The man is obscene. (*To* Brichot.) Take him out of the room to smoke a cigarette with you, so that my husband can warn our young man of the abyss that yawns at his feet.

333. *CHARLUS AT DOOR OF ROOM.*

The last guest has gone.

He turns from the door and walks the length of the room to Mme. Verdurin.

Charlus

There. Are you satisfied? You have every reason to be. You have had the Queen of Naples, the Princess of Taormina, the brother of the King of Bavaria, the three premier peers, countless duchesses, including my own sister-in-law, Oriane de Guermantes. If Vinteuil is Mahomet, we may say we have brought to him some of the least movable of mountains.

Mme. Verdurin *points to a fan on a chair.*

MME. VERDURIN

The Queen of Naples has left her fan.

CHARLUS

So she has. One would know it anywhere. It is uniquely hideous. Didn't Charlie play divinely? Where is he? I meant to present him to the Queen. And you yourself, my dear lady, played your part. Your name will not go unrecorded. The Duchesse de Duras was enchanted. She even asked me to tell you so. But where is Charlie? I haven't congratulated him.

BRICHOT

He's with the other musicians. Come and smoke a cigarette, Baron, for a few minutes. I would say you deserved one.

CHARLUS

I agree with you.

He walks with BRICHOT *towards an outer room.*

CHARLUS

What an immensely successful evening. He played like a god, didn't you think? Did you notice when that exquisite lock of hair came loose and fell onto his forehead? The Princess of Taormina, confronted by the message of the miraculous lock, suddenly realized it was music they were playing and not poker.

CHARLUS *and* BRICHOT *pass into the other room.*

334. *INT. ANOTHER ROOM.*

M. VERDURIN *and* MOREL *are standing in a corner.* MOREL *is pale.*

VERDURIN

If you like, we can go and ask my wife what she thinks. I give you my word of honor, I've said nothing to her about it. We shall see how she looks at it. You know very well she's a lady of the soundest judgment.

M. VERDURIN *opens the door carefully, sees that* CHARLUS *is not there, leads* MOREL *to* MME. VERDURIN.

VERDURIN (*to* MME. VERDURIN)
He would like to ask your advice about something.

MME. VERDURIN
I agree with my husband. You cannot tolerate this situation for another moment.

VERDURIN (*stammering*)
What . . . what do you mean? Tolerate what?

MME. VERDURIN
I guessed what you were saying to him. (*To* MOREL.) It is quite out of the question for you to endure any longer this degrading promiscuity with a tainted person whom nobody will have in her house. You are the talk of the Conservatoire. Another month of this life and your artistic future will be shattered.

MOREL
But I am . . . amazed . . . I . . . I've never heard anyone utter a word.

MME. VERDURIN
Then you are unique. His reputation is black. Blacker than black. I know for a fact he's been in prison. The police are watching him day and night. Even financially he can be of no use to you. He's the prey of every filthy blackmailer in Paris.

MOREL
I should never . . . have suspected it.

MME. VERDURIN
People are beginning to point you out, did you know that? It is essential that you wipe out this stain before it marks you for the rest of your life, before your life and your career are totally ruined!

Yes, yes.

MME. VERDURIN

He pretends to be your friend but he talks of you with
contempt. The other day someone said to him: "We
greatly admire your friend Morel." Do you know what
he said? "How can you call him my friend? We are not
of the same class, you must call him my creature."
Someone said he also used the word "servant," but I
can't vouch for that. But what he did say, what he
undoubtedly went on to say, was that your uncle was a
footman, a flunkey.

MOREL

What!

CHARLUS *and* BRICHOT *return.*

CHARLUS

Charlie! Well, how do you feel after your triumph? How
does it feel to be covered in glory?

MOREL

Leave me alone! Don't come near me! I know all about
you! I'm not the first person you've tried to corrupt!

CHARLUS *stands still, paralyzed.*
Silence.

MOREL

Pervert!

CHARLUS *looks at the others. No one moves.*

CHARLUS (*almost soundless*)

What has happened?

The VERDURINS *go through an arch into an outer
room.*
MOREL, *trembling, goes quickly to platform to pack
his violin.*
CHARLUS *stands still, looking at nothing.*
MOREL *suddenly notices the* QUEEN OF NAPLES,

143

*standing at the door of the room. She has clearly
overheard the preceding scene.*

336.   INT. THE OUTER ROOM.

> *The* VERDURINS. *They stand looking out of the
> window.*

MME. VERDURIN (*smirking*)

I think Charlus should sit down. He's tottering, he'll be
on the floor in a minute.

> MOREL *comes through the arch.*

MOREL

Isn't that lady the Queen of Naples?

> *They turn to look.*

MME. VERDURIN

It is.

> *The* QUEEN *can be seen talking quietly to* CHARLUS.

MOREL

The Baron was going to introduce me . . .

MME. VERDURIN

I'll introduce you. She's charming.

> *They move into the room and stand in front of the*
> QUEEN. MME. VERDURIN *curtsies.*

MME. VERDURIN

I am Madame Verdurin, Your Majesty. Your Majesty
does not remember me.

QUEEN OF NAPLES (*distantly*)

Quite well.

> *The* QUEEN *picks up her fan and offers* CHARLUS *her
> arm.*

QUEEN OF NAPLES

You look ill, my dear cousin. Lean on my arm. It once
held the rabble at bay at Gaeta. It will serve as a rampart
for you, now.

CHARLUS *takes her arm.*

They both walk slowly from the room.

The VERDURINS *and* MOREL *stare after them.*

MARCEL *watches.*

337.   *EXT. MARCEL'S FLAT. NIGHT.*

MARCEL *stands on the pavement looking up.*
A light shines from his flat.

338.   *INT. SITTING ROOM. NIGHT.*

ALBERTINE *reading.* MARCEL *enters, in his fur coat.*

MARCEL

Hullo. You're still up.

ALBERTINE

Yes.

MARCEL

Guess where I've just been. To the Verdurins'.

She throws down the book.

ALBERTINE

I thought as much.

Pause.

MARCEL

Why does that annoy you so much?

ALBERTINE

Annoy me? What do you mean? Why should I care
where you've been? It's all the same to me. Was
Mademoiselle Vinteuil there?

He sits down.

Pause.

ALBERTINE

How was the septet?

MARCEL

How do you know about the septet?

145

ALBERTINE

Everyone knows. It's not a secret.

MARCEL

I didn't know.

Pause.

ALBERTINE

Did Morel play well?

MARCEL

Have you had any contact with Morel?

ALBERTINE

Contact? Of course not. I hardly know him.

MARCEL

Then how did you hear about the septet?

ALBERTINE

I think it must have been Andrée who told me. She knows Morel quite well.

Pause.

MARCEL

The septet was wonderful. It gave me a happiness I have felt . . . rarely.

Pause.

MARCEL

Léa was there. The actress.

ALBERTINE

How odd.

MARCEL

She's a friend of Morel.

ALBERTINE

Is she?

MARCEL

She sent you her best wishes.

ALBERTINE

Did she? How odd. I hardly know her. We went to see

her act once last year and went round to her dressing room afterwards, to say hullo. That's all.

Pause.

MARCEL

Who went?

ALBERTINE

Oh, a few of us.

Pause.

MARCEL

You knew that Mademoiselle Vinteuil was expected at the Verdurins' this afternoon, didn't you?

ALBERTINE

Oh, these questions! (*Shrugging.*) Yes, I knew that.

MARCEL

Can you swear to me that it was not in order to renew your relations with her that you wanted to go there?

ALBERTINE

I never had any relations with her.

MARCEL

Can you swear to me that the pleasure of seeing her again had nothing to do with your wanting to be there?

ALBERTINE

No, I can't swear that. It would have given me great pleasure to see her again.

MARCEL

Listen . . . this evening I learned that what you had told me about Mademoiselle Vinteuil—

ALBERTINE

Was a lie. Yes. Yes, I did lie when I pretended to know her and her friend well, when I called them my two big sisters. But you see I thought you found me so boring, I thought if I told you I knew the family and knew about Vinteuil's music, you'd think better of me, you'd find me more interesting. When I lie to you, it is always out of affection for you! I've only met them about twice, in fact. I invented the story because I'm out of my depth with all these smart people you know—I haven't any money in the world—I'm absolutely poor . . .

He studies her.

MARCEL

That's silly. I have money. If you want to, you can give a dinner party for the Verdurins, for instance, any time you like.

ALBERTINE

Oh God! Thank you for nothing. A dinner party for those bores? (*Murmurs swiftly.*) I'd much rather you left me alone for once in a way so that I can go and get myself—

She stops abruptly.

MARCEL

What did you say?

ALBERTINE

Nothing . . . the Verdurins . . . the dinner.

MARCEL

No. You were saying something else. You stopped. Why did you stop?

ALBERTINE

Because I felt my request was unfair.

MARCEL

What request?

ALBERTINE

To be able to give a dinner party.

MARCEL

You didn't request it.

ALBERTINE

It's not right to take advantage of the fact that you have money. It's wrong.

Pause.

MARCEL

I didn't understand what you were saying. I didn't catch exactly what you said. You wanted to get—

ALBERTINE

Oh leave me alone, please!

MARCEL

But why? Why can't you finish . . . ?

ALBERTINE

I didn't know what I was saying. I was going to say— words I heard once, in the street. I don't even know what they mean. Just came into my head. It means nothing. I don't know what I meant.

MARCEL *looks at her in bewilderment.*

ALBERTINE

I'm just so upset that you went to the Verdurins' without telling me. You've deceived me and insulted me. I think I'll go to bed.

She goes.

He sits still.

Silence.

The camera remains on him for some moments.

339. *IMAGE OF ALBERTINE.*

She stops talking abruptly.

340. *MARCEL IN CHAIR.*

He closes his eyes, clenches them in pain.

341. *INT. ALBERTINE'S BEDROOM.*

She is looking at herself in a mirror.

MARCEL *comes in.*

MARCEL

Albertine, I think we should part. I want you to leave, first thing in the morning.

ALBERTINE

In the morning?

MARCEL

We have been happy. Now we're unhappy. It's quite simple.

ALBERTINE

I'm not unhappy.

MARCEL

Never see me again. It's best.

ALBERTINE

You are the only person I care for.

MARCEL

I've always wanted to go to Venice. Now I shall go. Alone.

Silence.

MARCEL

How many times have you lied to me?

Pause.

ALBERTINE

Well, I should have told you, when we were speaking about Léa just now, that I once took a three-week trip with her, it was before I knew you, but it was quite innocent, she behaved perfectly properly, she was just quite fond of me, that's all, as a daughter. I didn't tell you because I thought it might upset you, but absolutely nothing happened, nothing at all, I swear to you.

She looks about the room.

ALBERTINE

I can't believe I shall never see this room again. It seems impossible.

MARCEL

You were unhappy here.

ALBERTINE

No. It's now I shall be unhappy.

Where will you go?

I don't know. I shall have to think. Back to my aunt's, I suppose.

Pause.

Would you like us ... to try again ... for a few more weeks?

Yes. I would.

A few more weeks.

Yes. I think we should.

342. INT. MARCEL'S BEDROOM.

> MARCEL *alone in his room, sitting still.*
>
> *Suddenly the sound of a window being opened violently, from* ALBERTINE'S *room.*
>
> *He looks round sharply.*

343. INT. CORRIDOR. NIGHT. (SAME AS SHOT NO. 301.)

> *The corridor is dark.*
> MARCEL'S *door opens. He walks down the corridor to stand outside* ALBERTINE'S *room. He listens.*
> *Silence.*

344. INT. MARCEL'S BEDROOM. MORNING.

> MARCEL *in bed.* FRANÇOISE *comes in.*

I didn't know what to do. Mademoiselle Albertine asked me for her trunks—at seven o'clock this morning. You

were asleep. I didn't want to wake you. You say never to
wake you. She packed. She's gone. She left.

He stares at her.

MARCEL

You were quite right not to wake me.

345. *MARCEL'S EYES.*

346. *THE EYES OF GILBERTE AT TANSONVILLE.*

347. *THE EYES OF THE DUCHESSE DE GUER-
MANTES IN THE STREET.*

348. *THE EYES OF ODETTE IN THE AVENUE DES
ACACIAS.*

349. *THE EYES OF MOTHER IN THE BEDROOM AT
COMBRAY.*

350. *THE EYES OF MARCEL IN THE LAVATORY AT
COMBRAY.*

351. *THE EYES OF MARCEL.*

352. *INT. MARCEL'S BEDROOM. PARIS. 1902.*

FRANÇOISE *handing him a telegram.*

He opens it, reads it.

He lets it drop.

FRANÇOISE *picks it up, reads it.*
She gasps and puts her hand to her mouth.
She looks at MARCEL.
*She puts the telegram on the table and slowly leaves
the room.*

The camera stays on MARCEL *who remains still, his
face blank.*

353. *EXT. FIELD. DAY.*

> *A riderless horse gallops away from the camera.*
>
> *The camera pulls back slightly to reveal the suggestion of the broken body of a girl.*

354. *INT. MARCEL'S FLAT. THE HALL. DAY.*

> *The empty hall.*

355. *INT. THE DINING ROOM. EVENING.*

> *The empty dining room.*

356. *INT. MARCEL'S ROOM. NIGHT.*

> MARCEL *sitting, his face blank.*

357. *INT. THE HALL. NIGHT.*

> *The door of* ALBERTINE'*s room is ajar.*
> *The hall is empty.*
> *Silence.*

358. *INT. MARCEL'S ROOM. DAY.*

> MARCEL *sitting, his face blank.*

359. *C.U. ANDRÉE.*

> MARCEL'*s voice over.*

MARCEL (V.O.)
Now that she's dead . . . I can ask you quite frankly . . .
You like women, don't you?

> ANDRÉE *smiles.*

ANDRÉE
Yes. I do.

360. *INT. MARCEL'S ROOM. TWO SHOT. DAY. 1902.*

MARCEL
You knew Mademoiselle Vinteuil . . . well, didn't you?

ANDRÉE

No, not her, actually. Her friend.

Pause.

MARCEL

I have known for years, of course, of the things you used to do with Albertine.

ANDRÉE

I never did anything with Albertine.

361. INT. MARCEL'S ROOM. NIGHT.

MARCEL *and* ANDRÉE *sit in different positions in the room.* ANDRÉE *wears a different dress.*

MARCEL

I find you very attractive. Perhaps because of the things you did with Albertine. I want what she had.

ANDRÉE

That's impossible. You're a man.

Pause.

ANDRÉE

She was so passionate. Remember that day you lost your key, when you brought home syringa? You nearly caught us. It was so dangerous, we knew you would be home any minute, but she needed it, she had to have it. I pretended she hated the scent of syringa, do you remember? She was behind the door. She said the same thing, to keep you away from her, so that you wouldn't smell me on her.

362. INT. MARCEL'S ROOM. DAY.

MARCEL *and* ANDRÉE *sitting.*

ANDRÉE

You *want* me to say it, don't you? But I won't say things which aren't true. Albertine detested that sort of thing. I can swear it. I can swear that I never did that sort of thing with Albertine.

363. *INT. MARCEL'S ROOM. NIGHT.*

> MARCEL *and* ANDRÉE *sitting.*

ANDRÉE

She and Morel understood each other at once. He procured girls for her. He would seduce the girl first, and then, when the girl was absolutely under his control, he'd hand her over to Albertine, and they'd both enjoy the girl together.

Pause.

ANDRÉE

Léa had her many times at the baths at Balbec, last summer in Balbec. I remember once being with her and some laundresses—oh quite young—by the banks of a river near Balbec. I remember one girl—very sweet she was too—doing something to Albertine—I can't possibly tell you what—and she cried out: "Oh how heavenly." "Oh how heavenly" . . . quivering, naked, on the grass.

364. *INT. MARCEL'S ROOM. DAY.*

> MARCEL *and* ANDRÉE *sitting.*

ANDRÉE

The people who have told you these stories about Albertine were lying to you . . . can't you understand that?

MARCEL

No one has told me any stories.

365. *INT. MARCEL'S ROOM. NIGHT.*

ANDRÉE

She hoped that you would rescue her, that you would marry her. She loved you. She felt in her heart her

155

obsession was a sort of criminal lunacy. I think she might quite possibly have killed herself, out of despair.

366. *LARGE PROFILE. SWANN.*

> Swann's *voice over.*

> SWANN (V.O.)
> To think I have wasted years of my life, that I have longed for death, that the greatest love I have ever known has been for a woman who did not appeal to me, who was not my type.

367. *EXT. GRAND CANAL. VENICE. DAY. 1903.*

> *Wintery, desolate.*
> MARCEL *in a gondola approaching a palazzo.*

368. MOTHER FRAMED IN A WINDOW.

> *She is sitting on a balcony of the palazzo reading.*
> *She looks up from her book to see* MARCEL *in the gondola.*

369. *THE GONDOLA ARRIVING AT THE LANDING.*

> MARCEL *steps out of the gondola, looks up to see his mother. His face is expressionless.*

370. C.U. MOTHER.

> *She looks down with an expression of helpless love.*

371. *EXT. SAINT MARK'S SQUARE. DAY.*

> *The square is desolate.*
> MARCEL *and* MOTHER *sitting among empty tables outside a café.*
> MOTHER *is reading. She glances from her book at* MARCEL.

372. EXT. VENICE. EVENING.

> Gondolas swaying near Saint Mark's Church.

373. INT. SAINT MARK'S CHURCH.

> Sounds of two pairs of feet walking over the cobbles.
> They stop.
>
> The camera pans up to the blue mosaics of the
> church.

374. EXT. PARIS STREET. 1915.

> Searchlights in the sky, air raid sirens.
>
> The camera pans down to a rather derelict street.
> There is a general blackout.
>
> MARCEL (35) walks alone into the street.
> Lights glint through the shutters of what appears to
> be a small hotel.
> He walks towards it, stops.
>
> The door of the hotel has suddenly opened. An
> officer comes out.
>
> In the flash of light MARCEL recognizes SAINT-LOUP
> (37). SAINT-LOUP hesitates a moment, and then
> strides away.

375. INT. HOTEL FOYER.

> MARCEL enters.
>
> A MAN at the desk in evening clothes is whispering
> to the MANAGER.

MANAGER

Impossible, sir. Next week perhaps. I'll see what I can
do.

> In an anteroom MARCEL notices a group of young
> soldiers lounging about, playing dice, and also one or
> two young civilians.

The Man *in evening clothes turns from the desk,
glances quickly at* Marcel, *leaves the hotel.*

Marcel *walks slowly to the desk.*
From outside, gunfire in the distance.

> MARCEL

I'd like a room, until the raid's over.

> MANAGER

Yes, yes. We can do that. Is there . . . anything else I can
get you, sir?

> MARCEL

A bottle of champagne.

> MANAGER

Ah.

376. INT. HOTEL. LANDING.

The MANAGER, *carrying a tray with a bottle of
champagne, leads* MARCEL *to a room.*
They go in.

377. INT. ROOM.

The room is very bare.
The MANAGER *opens the bottle and pours a glass.*
MARCEL *sits down.*

> MARCEL

Thank you.

> MANAGER

When you're . . . ready for anything else, sir, just ring,
and I'll be up to see what you require.

He goes out.

MARCEL *sits drinking.*
Gunfire in the distance.
*He suddenly notices an object lying on the floor by
the foot of the bed. He goes to it, picks it up.*

158

It is a Croix de Guerre.

The gunfire stops. In the silence MARCEL *becomes aware of faint cries from somewhere in the hòtel. He puts the Croix de Guerre in his pocket and goes out of the room.*

378. INT. LANDING.

MARCEL *walks in the direction of the cries.*

379. STAIRS TO THE NEXT FLOOR.

MARCEL *reaches the top of the stairs.*
The cries are nearer.
He walks towards a room at the end of the corridor.

A VOICE
Have mercy, have mercy, you're killing me!

ANOTHER VOICE
Mercy? For a filthy old bastard like you?

Cracks of a whip. Shouts of pain.
MARCEL *notices a small oval-shaped window looking into the room, the curtain half-pulled.*
He looks in.

380. THE ROOM FROM MARCEL'S P.O.V.

CHARLUS (68), *chained to the bed, naked, being beaten by a* YOUNG MAN *with a whip.*

The door opens. JUPIEN (66) *comes in.*

JUPIEN
Everything all right, Baron?

CHARLUS
Can we have a word?

JUPIEN
Go downstairs, Maurice.

159

Yes, Monsieur Jupien.

MAURICE *bows shyly to* CHARLUS *and goes out.*

CHARLUS

He hasn't got his heart in it, that fellow. I know he's doing his best but he's simply not brutal enough, nowhere near brutal enough. He doesn't mean it, you see! He's pretending.

JUPIEN

Oh, I'm so sorry. I have a butcher's assistant downstairs. An absolute thug. He nearly killed a defrocked priest up here the other day. Would you like him?

CHARLUS

He sounds a better bet.

JUPIEN

Shall I unchain you while I look for him?

381. *C.U. CHARLUS.*

CHARLUS (*heavily*)

No. Leave me chained.

382. *EXT. CORRIDOR.*

JUPIEN *comes out of the room.*
MARCEL *lets himself be seen.* JUPIEN *stares at him.*
MARCEL *glances in at* CHARLUS *again, and then walks
down the stairs in silence.*
JUPIEN *follows.*

JUPIEN

I'm . . . very surprised to see you here, sir.

MARCEL

I came in to shelter from the raid.

383. *INT. MARCEL'S HOTEL ROOM.*

MARCEL *and* JUPIEN *enter.*

MARCEL *pours himself another glass of champagne.*
JUPIEN *stands looking at him.*

MARCEL

You own this . . . hotel, I take it?

JUPIEN

Yes, but I don't want you to misjudge me. The profit's
very small. I have to let rooms to respectable people as
well, sometimes. The running costs are high. Equip-
ment, overheads, labor, et cetera. No, you see, I took
this house for the Baron, to amuse him in his old age.
I'm fond of him. As for the lads, the Baron enjoys their
companionship, as much as anything else. He often plays
cards with them. I must get my thug for him. Actually
he's not a thug. He's a sweet young thing who sends
most of the money he earns here home to his mother.

MARCEL

I think you should have this. It was lying on the floor in
this room.

He hands JUPIEN *the Croix de Guerre.*

JUPIEN

My goodness. A Croix de Guerre.

MARCEL

Perhaps you might return it to its owner.

JUPIEN

Yes, yes. Of course.

384. *EXT. PARK AT TANSONVILLE. DAY. 1915.*

The pond, seen through a gap in the hedge.
A fishing line rests by the side of the pond, the float
bobbing in the water.

MARCEL *and* GILBERTE *appear and walk to the side*
of the pond. They are both aged thirty-five and both
dressed in mourning.

Two days after Robert was killed I received a package, sent anonymously. It contained his Croix de Guerre. There was no note of explanation, nothing. The package was posted in Paris.

Pause.

GILBERTE

Isn't that strange?

MARCEL

Yes.

GILBERTE

He never mentioned, in any letter, that it had been lost, or stolen.

385. *INT. DRAWING ROOM. SWANN'S HOUSE AT TANSONVILLE. EVENING.*

MARCEL *and* GILBERTE *stand by the windows.*

GILBERTE

I loved him. But we had grown unhappy. He had another woman, or other women, I don't know.

MARCEL

Other women?

GILBERTE

Yes. He had some secret life, which he never confessed to me, but I know he found it irresistible.

386. *EXT. PARK. TANSONVILLE. MORNING.*

MARCEL *and* GILBERTE *walking.*

GILBERTE

Do you remember your childhood at Combray?

MARCEL

Not really.

GILBERTE

How long is it since you've been back?

MARCEL

Oh, a very long time. It's changed.

GILBERTE

The war has changed everything.

MARCEL

No, it's nothing to do with the war.

GILBERTE

But are you saying that these paths, these woods, the village, excite nothing in you?

MARCEL

Nothing. They mean nothing to me. It's all dead. I remember almost nothing of it.

Pause.

MARCEL

I remember seeing you, through the hedge. I adored you.

GILBERTE

Did you? I wish you'd told me at the time. I thought you were delicious.

MARCEL *stares at her.*

MARCEL

What?

GILBERTE

I longed for you. Of course I was quite precocious, I suppose, then. I used to go to some ruins—at Roussainville—with some girls and boys, from the village, in the dark. We were quite wicked. I longed for you to come there. I remember, that moment through the hedge, I tried to let you know how much I wanted you, but I don't think you understood.

He laughs.

Why are you laughing?

MARCEL

Because I didn't understand. I've understood very little.
I've been too . . . preoccupied . . . with other matters . . .
To be honest, I have wasted my life.

387. INT. SANATORIUM. MARCEL'S ROOM. DAY. 1917.

The sanatorium is in a large château by the side of a lake.

MARCEL sits still, alone, in the large room. He is thirty-seven.
He wears his coat.
He is motionless as an owl.

388. INT. SANATORIUM. CORRIDOR.

A doctor in a white coat passes the camera in foreground.

At the very end of the long corridor we see MARCEL standing.

389. INT. SANATORIUM. MARCEL'S ROOM.

MARCEL sitting still.
Birds wheel at the window.
He does not hear them.

390. EXT. SANATORIUM. THE LAKE.

MARCEL sitting on a bench with his back to the lake.
In the distance figures in white coats.

391. EXT. COUNTRYSIDE. DAY. 1921.

A train, still.

A railwayman walks along the side of the train,

tapping the wheels with a hammer. The sound
echoes.

392. INT. RAILWAY CARRIAGE.

      Marcel *alone. He is forty-one.*

      A line of trees in background.

      A window is open but the sound of the hammer is
      not heard.

393. INT. MARCEL'S FLAT. 1921.

      His hands opening an envelope.
      He takes out a card.
      It is an invitation to an afternoon party given by the
      Prince *and* Princesse de Guermantes.
      He puts the invitation on his desk.

394. FLASH OF THE PRINCESSE DE GUERMANTES AT
      HER BOX AT THE OPERA.

395. EXT. PRINCE DE GUERMANTES'S HOUSE. AVE-
      NUE DU BOIS.

      Marcel *walking towards it.*
      Carriages, cars, crowds of chauffeurs.
      A car is driving towards the house. Marcel *steps in*
      front of it. The chauffeur shouts. Marcel *steps back,*
      trips over uneven paving stones.

      He sways, recovers balance, puts his foot back on the
      lower paving stone.

396. *Very dim quick flash of Venice.*

397. Marcel*'s face.*

398. *EXT. PRINCE DE GUERMANTES'S HOUSE.*

> MARCEL *stands still.*
>
> *He sways back again and forward.*
>
> *He remains still.*
>
> *He sways back again and forward.*
>
> *In background chauffeurs regarding him curiously, with amusement.*
>
> MARCEL *sways back.*

399. *Blue glow.*

400. *Chauffeurs.*

401. *Blue mosaics in Saint Mark's Church.*

402. MARCEL's *face.*

403. *INT. PRINCE DE GUERMANTES'S HOUSE.*

> *The doors of the Guermantes' house have been opened.*
>
> *Camera follows* MARCEL *into the house and up the stairs.*
>
> *Sound of music from behind closed doors.*
>
> *A* BUTLER *on the landing comes forward.*

BUTLER

The Princess has given orders for the doors to be kept shut until the music has ended. Will you wait in the library, sir?

404. *INT. THE LIBRARY.*

> MARCEL *enters the library and sits down.*
>
> *He is alone apart from a* WAITER *who stands at the table with refreshments.*

The WAITER *inadvertently knocks a spoon against a plate.*

405. *Open countryside, a line of trees, seen from a railway carriage.*

    Sound of a hammer tapping a wheel.

406. *The* WAITER *with the spoon.*

    Sound of hammer over.

407. *The train in the clearing.*

    RAILWAYMAN *tapping wheel.*

408. MARCEL *in carriage. No sound.*

409. MARCEL *in library. Sound of hammer.*

    MARCEL *looks down at the table by him. On it are some petits fours and a glass of orange juice.*

    He drinks, wipes mouth with starched napkin. The napkin crackles.

410. *Flash of blue sky seen through a window.*

411. MARCEL *with napkin at his mouth.*

412. *Full still frame of the sea and sky seen from a high window, a starched towel being placed on a towel rack in the foreground.*

413. MARCEL *and the* WAITER, *still.*

414. *Water pipes in the library.*

    Shrill noise of water running through pipes.

415. *Flash of silver cutlery glittering on table.*

416. MARCEL's *face.*

417. *The dining room at Balbec. Empty. Sunset.*

> *The tables are laid. In the distance sounds of a steamer.*

418. MARCEL *in library.*

> *Sounds of a steamer over.*

419. INT. DRAWING ROOM. PRINCE DE GUERMANTES'S HOUSE. 1921.

> *The drawing room doors open.*
> *Camera enters with* MARCEL, *who hesitates.*
>
> *Hundreds of faces, some of which turn towards him, grotesquely made up, grotesquely old.*
>
> *He walks into the room. Voices. Faces. The wigs and makeup, combined with the extreme age of those who with difficulty stand, sit, gesture, laugh, give the impression of grotesque fancy dress.*

420. IMAGE OF VENICE APPEARS ON THE SCREEN AND IMMEDIATELY FADES.

421. THE DUCHESSE DE GUERMANTES (63) AND MARCEL.

DUCHESSE

It's years, years, years. How many years? When was it exactly? Where have you been? You haven't changed a bit, have you? Well, just a little perhaps. I'm very long in the tooth, aren't I? Well, of course I'm no chicken.

422. SEA AND SKY AND THE WINDOW AT BALBEC APPEAR ON THE SCREEN AND IMMEDIATELY FADE.

423. *THE DUCHESSE AND MARCEL.*

> *A very old bent man passes.*

MARCEL

Who is that?

DUCHESSE

The Comte d'Argencourt. Do you remember him? Had a terrible reputation. Mostly with footmen.

MARCEL (*looking after* D'ARGENCOURT)

I can't believe it.

DUCHESSE

Well, he's changed, of course. Do you know you're probably my only friend here, my truest friend? You met everyone at my house, didn't you? You met Swann first at my house.

MARCEL

I knew him a little, when I was a child.

DUCHESSE

His daughter's here somewhere, Gilberte. Do you know her?

MARCEL

Not very well.

DUCHESSE

She never loved Robert, you know, never. She's a bitch.

424. *THE COUNTRYSIDE AND LINE OF TREES FROM TRAIN WINDOW APPEAR ON THE SCREEN AND IMMEDIATELY FADE.*

425. *THE DUCHESSE AND MARCEL.*

MARCEL

Where is the Princess?

DUCHESSE (*pointing*)

She's there, over there.

MARCEL *looks in the direction of her finger and sees* MME. VERDURIN, *who is eighty-one.*

The camera focuses on MME. VERDURIN, *momentarily.*

MARCEL

That's not the Princess.

DUCHESSE

Oh yes it is. She was once called Verdurin. My darling cousin is dead. Mother Verdurin is the new Princess, my new cousin. Can you believe it? The Prince found her money very useful.

426. *THE BALBEC DINING ROOM AT SUNSET APPEARS ON THE SCREEN AND IMMEDIATELY FADES.*

427. *M. DE CAMBREMER AND MARCEL.*

M. DE CAMBREMER *is seventy-five, his face pockmarked and distorted.*

M. DE CAMBREMER

Someone told me you've been in a sanatorium for years, my dear fellow. Do you still suffer from choking fits? I mean has there been any improvement?

MARCEL

Not much.

M. DE CAMBREMER

They become much less frequent with age though, surely? And after all you're getting on. (*Absently.*) My sister suffers much less from them, now.

428. *MARCEL ALONE.*

He looks closely at people in the room and the

camera pans over limping crooked men, half-para-
lyzed women, bodies trembling, faces caked with
makeup.

429. SUDDEN CLOSE UP OF THE VICOMTESSE DE
SAINT-FIACRE.

She is a cocaine addict. Her face is haggard. She
grins permanently.

VICOMTESSE (*into camera*)
Hullo.

430. MARCEL.

He gazes at a group of people who from a distance
appear to be young.
He draws nearer and sees that the faces are actually
wrinkled and greasy, the eyes tiny behind pouches of
flesh.

BRICHOT *passes, totally blind. He is eighty-four.*

431. ODETTE SITTING ON SOFA SURROUNDED BY
YOUNG MEN.

She is sixty-four, but remains beautiful.

432. MOREL ENTERS THE ROOM.

He is forty-one.
He is greeted warmly.
The PRINCESSE DE GUERMANTES (*Mme. Verdurin*)
calls across the room.

PRINCESSE DE GUERMANTES
Ah here's the great musician, the great man!

MOREL *goes towards her and the* PRINCE DE GUER-
MANTES, *who is seventy-five.*

433. *MME. DE CAMBREMER (70) AND THE DU-CHESSE DE GUERMANTES.*

MARCEL *in background.*

MME. DE CAMBREMER

What has become of the Marquise d'Arpajon?

DUCHESSE DE GUERMANTES

She died.

MME. DE CAMBREMER

No no, you're confusing her with the Comtesse d'Arpajon.

DUCHESSE DE GUERMANTES

Certainly not. The Marquise is dead too. About a year ago.

MME. DE CAMBREMER

But I was at a musical party at her house about a year ago.

DUCHESSE DE GUERMANTES

Well she's quite dead, I can promise you. I'm not surprised you haven't heard. She died in a quite unremarkable way.

434. *GILBERTE (41) AND MARCEL.*

GILBERTE

I can't understand what you're doing at a party like this. Why don't we dine together tonight in a restaurant?

MARCEL

Yes, of course . . . if you won't find it compromising to dine alone with a young man.

GILBERTE *laughs.*
One or two other people turn, smiling at this remark.

MARCEL

An old man.

435. *CLOSE SHOT. THE PRINCESSE DE GUER-*
   MANTES.

> *She laughs wildly and adjusts her monocle.*

GILBERTE (V.O.)

She's my aunt now, you know.

436. *MARCEL AND GILBERTE.*

GILBERTE

I must tell you, I have a great friend now who knew you
once, I believe. Her name's Andrée.

MARCEL

Yes, I knew her.

GILBERTE

She's here somewhere, with her husband. Oh no, there
she is, over there, talking to Morel.

> MOREL *and* ANDRÉE (43) *across the room talking.*

437. *MARCEL AND RACHEL.*

> RACHEL (44) *looks much older than she actually is.*

RACHEL

No, I can see you don't remember me.

MARCEL

Yes yes, I do.

RACHEL

Who am I then?

MARCEL

I . . .

RACHEL

I'll tell you. We met backstage once in a theater with a
friend of yours. He was madly in love with me. Do you
remember?

MARCEL

Oh yes. Yes I do.

He adored me.

438. THE DUC DE GUERMANTES SITTING WITH ODETTE ON A SOFA.

The DUC *appears to be as handsome and majestic as ever. His hair is white. He is seventy-five.*
Young men are talking to ODETTE.
Occasionally the DUC *speaks.* ODETTE *turns sharply to him and then back smiling to the young men.*

439. THE DUCHESSE AND MARCEL.

DUCHESSE

You've met Rachel. Do you know she's the greatest actress in Paris? Oh by the way, my husband is having another affair at the age of seventy-five! Remarkable isn't it? But we're still quite fond of each other.

440. GILBERTE AND MARCEL.

GILBERTE

The Duc de Guermantes is a great admirer of my mother. He is in her house all the time. She doesn't age at all, does she?

MARCEL

No, not at all.

GILBERTE

People have always fallen in love with my mother.

441. THE DUC DE GUERMANTES WALKING TO THE DOOR.

Now he is standing, we realize his age.
He finds great difficulty in walking, gropes along, wipes his brow, totters.

174

ODETTE

Sit down by me. I'm delighted to meet you. You knew my first husband well, didn't you?

MARCEL

Your *first* husband?

ODETTE

Charles Swann. I'm Madame de Forcheville now. But Monsieur de Forcheville is dead too, now. But you did know Charles.

MARCEL

Yes, in my childhood, a little.

ODETTE

I know you're a writer. Oh the things I could tell you, the material I could give you. Are you interested in love, I mean do you write about it? But what else is there to write about? All my lovers have been so ridden with jealousy. Charles was unbelievably jealous. But he was so intelligent. I could never love a man who was unintelligent. I never loved Monsieur de Forcheville. He was quite commonplace, really. But I adored Charles, and we were so happy, most of the time. Charles always intended to write himself, you know, but (*she giggles*) I think he was too much in love with me to find the time.

443. *MARCEL STANDING ALONE.*

GILBERTE *approaches* MARCEL *with a* YOUNG GIRL *of sixteen. She is very lovely.*

GILBERTE

This is my daughter.

MLLE. DE SAINT-LOUP *smiles and inclines her head.* MARCEL *gazes at her.*

Suddenly all the sounds in the room die.
MLLE. DE SAINT-LOUP *speaks silently, smiling.*

Over this shot we hear the garden gate bell at Combray, "resilient, ferruginous, interminable, fresh and shrill."

The bell continues over the following shots:

444. *The vast room, the multitude of people, talking.*
     No sound.

445. MLLE. DE SAINT-LOUP *smiling.*

446. *The trees at Hudimesnil.*

447. *The steeples at Martinville.*

448. *Flash of yellow screen.*

449. *The river Vivonne at Combray.*

450. *The roofs of Combray.*

451. *The garden at Combray in the evening.*

452. *The bell at the garden gate.*

453. SWANN *opening the garden gate and departing.*

454. MARCEL *as a child looking out of his bedroom window.*
     The bell ceases.

455. *Vermeer's* View of Delft.

> *Camera moves in swiftly to the patch of yellow wall*
> *in the painting.*
>
> *Yellow screen.*

MARCEL'S VOICE OVER

It was time to begin.

Selected List of Grove Press Drama and Theater Paperbacks

E312 ARDEN, JOHN / Serjeant Musgrave's Dance / $2.45 [See also Modern British Drama, Henry Popkin, ed. GT614 / $5.95]

B109 ARDEN, JOHN / Three Plays: Live Like Pigs, The Waters of Babylon, The Happy Haven / $2.45

E127 ARTAUD, ANTONIN / The Theater and Its Double (Critical Study) / $2.95

E425 BARAKA, IMAMU AMIRI (LEROI JONES) / The Baptism and The Toilet / $2.45

E540 BARNES, PETER / The Ruling Class / $2.95

E471 BECKETT, SAMUEL / Cascando and Other Short Dramatic Pieces (Words and Music, Film, Play, Come and Go, Eh Joe, Endgame) / $1.95

E96 BECKETT, SAMUEL / Endgame / $1.95

E318 BECKETT, SAMUEL / Happy Days / $2.45

E226 BECKETT, SAMUEL / Krapp's Last Tape, plus All That Fall, Embers, Act Without Words I and II / $2.45

E33 BECKETT, SAMUEL / Waiting For Godot / $1.95 [See also Seven Plays of the Modern Theater, Harold Clurman, ed. GT422 / $4.95]

B79 BEHAN, BRENDAN / The Quare Fellow* and The Hostage**: Two Plays / $2.45 *[See also Seven Plays of the Modern Theater, Harold Clurman, ed. GT422 / $4.95] **[See also Modern British Drama, Henry Popkin, ed. GT614 / $5.95]

B117 BRECHT, BERTOLT / The Good Woman of Setzuan / $1.95

B80 BRECHT, BERTOLT / The Jewish Wife and Other Short Plays (In Search of Justice, The Informer, The Elephant Calf, The Measures Taken, The Exception and the Rule, Salzburg Dance of Death) / $1.65

B90 BRECHT, BERTOLT / The Mother / $1.45

B108 BRECHT, BERTOLT / Mother Courage and Her Children / $1.50

B333 BRECHT, BERTOLT / The Threepenny Opera / $1.45

B88 BRECHT, BERTOLT / The Visions of Simone Machard / $1.25

E517   BULGAKOV, MIKHAIL / Flight: A Play in Eight Dreams and Four Acts / $2.25

GT422 CLURMAN, HAROLD (Ed.) / Seven Plays of the Modern Theater / $4.95 (Waiting For Godot by Samuel Beckett, The Quare Fellow by Brendan Behan, A Taste of Honey by Shelagh Delaney, The Connection by Jack Gelber, The Balcony by Jean Genet, Rhinoceros by Eugene Ionesco, and The Birthday Party by Harold Pinter)

E159   DELANEY, SHELAGH / A Taste of Honey / $1.95 (See also Modern British Drama, Henry Popkin, ed., GT614 / $5.95, and Seven Plays of the Modern Theater, Harold Clurman, ed. GT422 / $4.95)

E402   DURRENMATT, FRIEDRICH / An Angel Comes to Babylon and Romulus the Great / $3.95

E612   DURRENMATT, FRIEDRICH / Play Strindberg / $1.95

E344   DURRENMATT, FRIEDRICH / The Visit / $2.75

E223   GELBER, JACK / The Connection / $2.45 [See also Seven Plays of the Modern Theater, Harold Clurman, ed. GT422 / $4.95]

E130   GENET, JEAN / The Balcony / $2.95 [See also Seven Plays of the Modern Theater, Harold Clurman, ed. GT422 / $4.95]

E208   GENET, JEAN / The Blacks: A Clown Show / $2.95

E577   GENET, JEAN / The Maids and Deathwatch: Two Plays / $2.95

E374   GENET, JEAN / The Screens / $1.95

E457   HERBERT, JOHN / Fortune and Men's Eyes / $2.95

B154   HOCHHUTH, ROLF / The Deputy / $2.95

E456   IONESCO, EUGENE / Exit the King / $2.95

E101   IONESCO, EUGENE / Four Plays (The Bald Soprano, The Lesson, The Chairs,* Jack, or The Submission) / $1.95 *[See also Eleven Short Plays of the Modern Theater, Samuel Moon, ed. B107 / $2.45]

E646   IONESCO, EUGENE / A Hell of a Mess / $3.95

E506   IONESCO, EUGENE / Hunger and Thirst and Other Plays / $1.95

E189   IONESCO, EUGENE / The Killer and Other Plays (Improvisation, or The Shepherd's Chameleon, Maid to Marry) / $2.45

E613   IONESCO, EUGENE / Killing Game / $1.95

E259   IONESCO, EUGENE / Rhinoceros* and Other Plays (The Leader, The Future is in Eggs, or It Takes All Sorts to Make a World) / $1.95 *[See also Seven Plays of the Modern Theater, Harold Clurman, ed. GT422 / $4.95]

E485   IONESCO, EUGENE / A Stroll in the Air and Frenzy for Two: Two Plays / $2.45

E119   IONESCO, EUGENE / Three Plays (Amédée, The New Tenant, Victims of Duty) / $2.95

E387   IONESCO, EUGENE / Notes and Counter Notes / $3.95

E633   LAHR, JOHN (Ed.) / Grove Press Modern Drama / $6.95 (The Caucasian Chalk Circle by Bertolt Brecht, The Toilet by Imamu Amiri Baraka (LeRoi Jones), The White House Murder Case by Jules Feiffer, The Blacks by Jean Genet, Rhinoceros by Eugene Ionesco, Tango by Slawomir Mrozek)

E433   MROZEK, SLAWOMIR / Tango / $1.95

E462   NICHOLS, PETER / Joe Egg / $2.95

E567   ORTON, JOE / What The Butler Saw / $2.40

E583   OSBORNE, JOHN / Inadmissible Evidence / $2.45

B354   PINTER, HAROLD / Old Times / $1.95

E315   PINTER, HAROLD / The Birthday Party* and The Room: Two Plays / $1.95 *[See also Seven Plays of the Modern Theater, Harold Clurman, ed. GT422 / $4.95]

E299   PINTER, HAROLD / The Caretaker* and The Dumb Waiter: Two Plays / $1.95 *[See also Modern British Drama, Henry Popkin, ed. GT422 / $5.95]

E411   PINTER, HAROLD / The Homecoming / $1.95

E432   PINTER, HAROLD / The Lover, Tea Party, The Basement: Three Plays / $1.95

E480   PINTER, HAROLD / A Night Out, Night School, Revue Sketches: Early Plays / $1.95

GT614 POPKIN, HENRY (Ed.) / Modern British Drama / $5.95 (A Taste of Honey by Shelagh Delaney, The Hostage by Brendan Behan, Roots by Arnold Wesker, Serjeant Musgrave's Dance by John Arden, One Way Pendulum by N. F. Simpson, The Caretaker by Harold Pinter)

E635   SHEPARD, SAM / The Tooth of Crime and Geography of a Horsedreamer / $3.95

E626   STOPPARD, TOM / Jumpers / $1.95

B319   STOPPARD, TOM / Rosencrantz and Guilderstern Are Dead / $1.95

E660   STOREY, DAVID / In Celebration / $2.95

Grove Press, Inc., 196 West Houston Street, New York, N.Y. 10014